LEADING *With* LOVE

About the Author:

Alexander Strauch has served as a teacher and pastor elder at Littleton Bible Chapel in Littleton, Colorado, for more than forty years. He and his wife, Marilyn, have four children and eight grandchildren.

Other books by Alexander Strauch include

Biblical Eldership:
An Urgent Call to Restore Biblical Church Leadership

The Study Guide to Biblical Eldership:
Twelve Lessons for Mentoring Men for Eldership

The New Testament Deacon: Minister of Mercy

The Hospitality Commands

Agape Leadership:
Lessons in Spiritual Leadership from the Life of R. C. Chapman
coauthored with Robert L. Peterson

Men and Women: Equal Yet Different

Meetings That Work

Love or Die: Christ's Wake-up Call to the Church

A Christian Leader's Guide to

LEADING *With* LOVE

Alexander Strauch

Lewis & Roth Publishers

Leading with Love
ISBN: 0936083212
Copyright © 2006 by Alexander Strauch. All rights reserved.

Editors: Amanda Sorenson and Shannon Wingrove
Cover design: Eric Anderson

Printed in the United States of America
Sixth Printing 2009

Library of Congress Control Number: 2005939228

To receive a free catalog of books published by Lewis and Roth Publishers, please call toll free 800-477-3239 or visit our website, *www.lewisandroth.org*.

Lewis and Roth Publishers
P. O. Box 469
Littleton, Colorado 80160

Contents

Connecting Love and Leadership

Pursue love....
1 Cor. 14:1

It is no exaggeration to say that the Bible is a book of love. The story of the gospel, "God so loved the world, that he gave his only Son" (John 3:16), is the greatest love story ever told. Because of God's great love for us, we are to love the Lord our God with all our heart, soul, mind, and strength and to love our neighbor as ourself (Mark 12:30-31). While it is true that this requirement to love God and neighbor is incumbent upon all true believers, I have focused my attention on the subject of love as it applies to Christian leaders and teachers. Here's why.

First, although Christianity is unmatched among the religions of the world in its teaching about God's love and the requirements of love for Christian believers, Christian leaders don't normally focus on love when they address leadership. Much good material has been written describing the leadership qualities of courage, resourcefulness, charisma, conviction, perseverance, visionary thinking, self-discipline, decisiveness. Yet few books on church leadership include anything about love. This is a tragic oversight since the New Testament makes it clear that love is indispensable to the gifts of leading and teaching. Indeed, the New Testament mandates that spiritual gifts be exercised in love. As Paul puts it, any attempt at leading and teaching apart from love is like "a noisy gong or a clanging cymbal" (1 Cor. 13:1). To have all of the above leadership qualities but not love spells total failure for a Christian leader (1 Cor. 13:1-3).

Second, leaders and teachers set the spiritual tone for the church. They have the power to create a more loving atmosphere within the local church. If they are lovers of God and lovers of people, their followers will more likely be lovers of God and people. If, however, leaders are self-centered, critical, proud, angry, and impersonal, the people will adopt these same ugly dispositions.

Over the years I have talked to many people who were dissatisfied with their local church but didn't know exactly why. In many of these cases, I believe the missing element was the kind of love envisioned in the New Testament. Failure to love is all too common and it creates a broad spectrum of problems, as evidenced by the strife-ridden church at Corinth. That is why Scripture insists that leaders and teachers be examples of love: "Let no one despise you for your youth, but set the believers an example in speech, in conduct, in love" (1 Tim. 4:12). Love is vital to the local church because love is "the life-breath of the church,"[1] essential to its evangelistic witness and spiritual growth (Eph. 4:16).

Third, in the church family people must work closely together as brothers and sisters in Christ in making decisions and accomplishing tasks. At times this is difficult. Much work within the local church (and among local churches) is done in group settings: elders' and deacons' meetings, staff meetings, board meetings, committee meetings, and all-church meetings. The longer we work together, the more we get to know one another's faults and annoying personality traits, which can make life together frustrating. Understanding the New Testament principles of love will significantly enhance healthy group leadership, group meetings, and congregational life as a whole. Without love, we cannot live and work in harmony.

> **"Love is the most attractive quality in the world. And it lies at the heart of Christianity."**
>
> **—Michael Green**

Fourth, there are many false ideas about love that need correction. In the name of love, Christians have been known to abandon their families, commit every sort of sexual sin, refuse to practice church discipline, and redefine God and salvation according to contemporary notions of love and tolerance. Instead of love being "the fulfillment of the law," it has been made the enemy of the law (Rom. 13:8-10). Instead of love abhorring "what is evil," it has been used to justify evil (Rom 12:9). In his classic work *Testaments of Love* Leon Morris states, "There is no end to the list of horrors that have been perpetrated in the name of love."[2]

Despite these drawbacks, I firmly believe that truly understanding what the Bible says about love would significantly improve the relational skills of our church leaders and teachers and greatly enhance their effectiveness in ministry. It would diminish senseless conflict and division, promote evangelism, and produce spiritually healthy churches. Most important, it would please the Lord.

This book, therefore, is written to leaders and teachers at every level of leadership within the local church. If you lead or teach people—as a Sunday school teacher, youth worker, women's or men's ministry leader, Bible study leader, administrator, music director, elder, deacon, pastor, evangelist, or missionary—love is indispensable to you and your ministry. As Michael Green so beautifully reminds us, "Love is the most attractive quality in the world. And it lies at the heart of Christianity."[3] For that reason, God requires that you and I lead and teach with love and continually grow in our love for Him and for all people.

Notes

1. William Kelly, *Notes on the First Epistle to the Corinthians* (London: Morrish, 1878), 220.
2. Leon Morris, *Testaments of Love* (Grand Rapids, Mich.: Eerdmans, 1981), 3.
3. Michael Green, *Evangelism through the Local Church* (Nashville: Thomas Nelson, 1992), 97.

Part One

Love Is Indispensable to Christian Leadership

Chapter 1

Five Minus One Equals Zero

I will show you a still more excellent way.
1 Cor. 12:31

Dwight L. Moody, the Billy Graham of the 19th century, tells of his life-changing encounter with the doctrine of love. It began when Henry Moorhouse, a twenty-seven-year-old British evangelist, preached at Moody's church for a week. To everyone's surprise, Moorhouse preached seven sermons in a row on John 3:16. To prove that "God so loved the world" he preached on the love of God from Genesis to Revelation. Moody's son records his father's description of the impact of Moorhouse's preaching:

> For six nights he had preached on this one text. The seventh night came, and he went into the pulpit. Every eye was upon him. He said, "Beloved friends, I have been hunting all day for a new text, but I cannot find anything so good as the old one; so we will go back to the third chapter of John and the sixteenth verse," and he preached the seventh sermon from those wonderful words, "God so loved the world." I remember the end of that sermon: "My friends," he said, "for a whole week I have been trying to tell you how much God loves you, but I cannot do it with this poor stammering tongue. If I could borrow Jacob's ladder and climb up into heaven and ask Gabriel, who stands in the presence of the Almighty, to tell me how much love the Father has for the world, all he could say would be: 'God so loved the world, that He gave His only begotten Son, that whosoever believeth in Him should not perish, but have everlasting life.'"[1]

Unable to hold back the tears as Moorhouse preached on the love of God in sending His only Son to die for sinners, Moody confessed:

> I never knew up to that time that God loved us so much. This heart of mine began to thaw out; I could not keep back the tears. It was like news from a far country: I just drank it in. So did the crowded congregation. I tell you there is one thing that draws above everything else in the world, and that is love.[2]

As a result of Moorhouse's influence, Moody began to study the doctrine of love. This changed his life and his preaching. He later said:

> I took up that word "Love," and I do not know how many weeks I spent in studying the passages in which it occurs, till at last I could not help loving people! I had been feeding on Love so long that I was anxious to do everybody good I came in contact with.
>
> I got full of it. It ran out my fingers. You take up the subject of love in the Bible! You will get so full of it that all you have got to do is to open your lips, and a flood of the Love of God flows out upon the meeting. There is no use trying to do church work without love. A doctor, a lawyer, may do good work without love, but God's work cannot be done without love.[3]

D. L. Moody could not have been more biblically correct when he said, "God's work cannot be done without love." That is the message of the most famous love chapter in the Bible, 1 Corinthians 13.

The More Excellent Way

It is universally agreed that Paul is the greatest pioneer missionary, scholar, teacher, evangelist, and hero of the faith. Yet he knew that all his brilliance, multi-giftedness, and sacrificial dedication meant nothing if it were not bathed fully in love. *No other New Testament writer spoke more about love or provided more practical leadership examples of love than Paul. Through the lifetime ministry and letters of Paul, God gave his church, and all its leaders and teachers, a model of loving leadership.* In all of Scripture nowhere is it more clearly and forcefully stated that love is indispensable to leading and teaching than in 1 Corinthians 13.

Paul wrote this passage in response to disruptions that arose in the church of Corinth regarding spiritual gifts. To correct the church's misguided views of spiritual gifts and its overall self-destructive way of behaving, Paul promised to show the Corinthians a "more excellent way" to live (1 Cor. 12:31). He wanted them to know there is something far more important than supernatural gifts, something that transcends the most excellent gifts and performances, something that if absent will render all gifts worthless. That something is love.

The love Paul speaks of is primarily love for fellow believers. This love was defined by Jesus Christ when he gave a new commandment to all his disciples to love one another "just as" he had loved them (John 13:34-35). This love gives itself in total self-sacrifice for the good of others. Jesus exemplified this new pattern of love by humbly washing the disciples' feet (John 13:4-17) and selflessly sacrificing his life on the cross for others. John puts it this

> **"There is no use trying to do church work without love. A doctor, a lawyer, may do good work without love, but God's work cannot be done without love."**
>
> **—D. L. Moody**

way, "By this we know love, that he laid down his life for us, and we ought to lay down our lives for the brothers [and sisters]" (1 John 3:16).

To silence any doubt that love is the "more excellent way" and to jolt the Corinthians' wrong thinking about spiritual gifts, Paul uses all his rhetorical skills to communicate with eloquence and force that love is the "more excellent way." He writes:

> And I will show you a still more excellent way. If I speak in the tongues of men and of angels, but have not love, I am a noisy gong or a clanging cymbal. And if I have prophetic powers, and understand all mysteries and all knowledge, and if I have all faith, so as to remove mountains, but have not love, I am nothing. If I give away all I have, and if I deliver up my body to be burned, but have not love, I gain nothing. (1 Cor. 12:31–13:3)

Let's take a close look at this passage to gain a clearer understanding of what it says.

Without Love
Even Heavenly Language Sounds Annoying

The purpose of spiritual gifts was to build up and unite the body. Yet the Corinthians' enthusiasm over the supernatural gift of tongues caused pride and disorder in the church body. The independent-minded Corinthians used their gifts for personal ego gratification, which caused division within the body.

To correct this distortion, Paul captures their attention by hypothetically picturing himself as "the world's most gifted tongues-speaker,"[4] being able to speak eloquently in "the tongues of men and of angels." Such a gift would have greatly impressed the Corinthians. But Paul declares that even if he had such an exalted experience because of heavenly giftedness, he would be "a noisy gong or a clanging cymbal"—that is, an annoying, loud, empty noise—if he did not act in love, as described in verses 4 through 7. The beauty of his miraculous speech would be distorted without the grace of love.

Paul isn't merely saying that his speech would be a clamorous noise, but that he himself would be a hollow, annoying sound. He would not be what he should be; he would be seriously deficient in his Christian life and not living according to the "more excellent way." The reason Paul would be an empty noise is that he would be a loveless tongue-speaker. He would be using the gift of tongues to glorify and serve himself rather than to serve or build up the church, which is the goal of love (1 Cor. 8:1).

When I teach on this passage, I often use a visual illustration. I pull out from behind the pulpit a steel pot and a hammer and begin to beat on the pot as I talk about spiritual gifts and the need for love. At first, people laugh. They think it is a marvelous illustration. But I keep it up. While I am banging on the pot, I keep talking about spiritual gifts. Soon

Knowledge without love inflates the ego and deceives the mind.

people aren't laughing or smiling anymore. They have had enough; they're annoyed and getting more agitated by the moment, but I keep banging. When it seems they can't stand it any longer, I stop and ask, "Are you annoyed? Are you enjoying this? Does it please you? Do you find it edifying? Would you like me to continue beating the pot for the remainder of the message?" No one wants me to continue beating the pot. At this point I remind them that this is what they are like to others and to God when they use their gifts apart from love. They are nothing more than "a noisy gong or a clanging cymbal."

Without Love
Knowing It All Helps No One

Paul next speaks of himself hypothetically as possessing the gift of prophecy in such full measure that he would know "all" mysteries and "all" knowledge. He would thus have the theological answers to all the mysteries of God that people crave to understand. He would be a walking, talking encyclopedia of knowledge.

Some people love to display their intellect and theological superiority. They are proud of their learning and speaking ability. Such pride had become a serious problem at Corinth. Some people were arrogant because of their knowledge and puffed up with self-importance. They wanted recognition for their prophetic insights and superior wisdom, and they looked down on others with lesser knowledge and giftedness. As a result of their arrogant misuse of knowledge, they harmed the church body (1 Cor. 8).

Knowledge without love inflates the ego and deceives the mind. It can lead to intellectual snobbery, an attitude of mockery and making fun of others' views, a spirit of contempt for those with lesser knowledge, and a demeaning way of dealing with people who disagree. I know of a pastor who had a phenomenal knowledge of the Bible but who hurt many people with his doctrinal scrutiny and divided his own congregation repeatedly until there was no one left but himself. He had a big head but a little heart. His theology was as clear as ice and twice as cold. Such is the path of one who has knowledge without love.

So Paul states that even if he had all-encompassing knowledge, apart from love he would be "nothing"—a spiritual zero. He insists that a loveless prophet, a loveless scholar, or a loveless teacher is worthless to the discipling of God's people. History confirms this, as John Short observes:

Loveless faith and loveless prophecy account for some of the more tragic pages in the Christian story through the ages. It has burned so-called heretics; it has stultified the sincere quest for truth; it has often been contentious and embittered; and it has often issued in the denial of Christian brotherhood to fellow believers.[5]

In a similar vein, George Sweeting, former president of Moody Bible Institute, makes this observation: "I have been keenly disappointed to find people more concerned about hidden mysteries than about needy people.... Too often Christians are concerned about hidden truth, but indifferent about loving difficult people."[6]

Only with love can knowledge be used according to the "more excellent way" to protect and build up the church (Eph. 4:11-16).

Without Love
Risk-taking Faith Is Worthless

The third spiritual gift Paul presents is faith (1 Cor. 12:9). He imagines himself possessing the most excellent gift of faith imaginable, "so as to remove mountains." Like Abraham, he would believe God for the impossible and actively trust Him to do miraculous works. He would be a powerhouse of prayer, a spiritual risk taker, a virtual George Muller,[7] greatly admired and sought by all. He would be a courageous David racing out in battle to kill the Philistine giant Goliath (1 Sam. 17: 32). But even with such a powerful spiritual gift, if love is not present, the gift becomes a means of glorifying oneself rather than serving others.

> **"Too often Christians are concerned about hidden truth, but indifferent about loving difficult people."**
>
> **—George Sweeting**

Some "miracle" workers on television may claim to do the impossible by faith, but they talk more about money, success, and themselves than about the people they supposedly help. Like the self-flaunting Pharisees, they want "to be seen by others" (Matt. 6:5). They love the praise of man and want to be revered as spiritual giants who do great things for God. They use their wonderful gifts to promote themselves, not the body of Christ.

I recall a radio preacher who spoke often of the marvelous things God was doing through his broadcasts and how God miraculously provided funds without his begging for money (which can be a subtle way of begging for money). But those who knew the man personally and worked for him saw things differently. They saw a man who was obsessed with money and public image. They saw his gift of faith being used to guarantee his own financial security. They saw a man who didn't care much at all for people but who cared a lot about himself.

No wonder Paul declares so emphatically that such a powerful gift without love is worth "nothing." Paul means what he says. Without love he knew he would be spiritually fruitless rather than a spiritual powerhouse.

Without love, the Christian leader is on the wrong path of the Christian life. But when faith is combined with love, the body of Christ is built up and advances forward on the royal road, the "more excellent way" of love.

Without Love
Giving All One's Money to the Poor
Is Unprofitable

Paul next considers giving away all his worldly possessions—his home, property, furniture, savings, and all the things he cherishes most—to feed the poor. He gives it all and reduces himself to abject poverty. Surely this is the ultimate, altruistic action. Wouldn't such giving be, by definition, *love*? Not necessarily. Paul makes it clear that the most extraordinary, self-sacrificing action can be done without love.

Self-sacrifice can be done for self-interest as illustrated by Ananias and Sapphira in the book of Acts. This couple sold their property and gave money to the apostles to distribute to the poor (Acts 5:1-11). However, they gave without love. They weren't really concerned about the needs of the poor, but about themselves. They didn't love God or their neighbor. Like the trumpet-blowing Pharisees whom Jesus condemned in the Sermon on the Mount (Matt. 6:1-5), Ananias and Sapphira gave in order to enhance their personal prestige in the sight of the church. They gave to receive the praise of people. Their love was hypocritical love (Rom. 12:9). They gave to the poor, but without the true, inner motivating power of love, so their giving profited them nothing. Although they gave money to the poor, they were spiritually bankrupt, and God rejected their gift.

Paul says, therefore, that if he gave all he owned to the poor but did so apart from love, it would be unproductive, useless, worthless, and of no eternal value. Even after such sacrifice he would be a spiritually bankrupt man. He would not be humbly serving others, but would be serving himself.

In contrast, when one is moved by love to meet the needs of the poor, giving all of one's possessions profits everyone. Such is the love that motivated the Lord Jesus Christ to give up the riches of heaven and become poor for us. For that reason, "God has highly exalted him and bestowed on him the name that is above every name" (Phil. 2:9). Jesus gave according to the "more excellent way."

Without Love
The Ultimate Sacrifice of One's Life
Is Pointless

Finally, Paul envisions himself as the ultimate hero of the faith. In an act of supreme sacrifice, he surrenders his body to the painful flames of martyrdom for Christ. Such a sacrifice would certainly inspire other believers to faithfulness, greater dedication, and courage. It would provide a powerful witness of the gospel to nonbelievers. But Paul warns us that even suffering and martyrdom for Christ can be done for the wrong reasons.

Some people take great pride in suffering for their faith. For others, it is worth dying in order to be remembered as a hero of the faith. In the early years of Christianity, becoming a martyr became at times a means of achieving great fame. One historian comments, "It soon was clear to all Christians that extraordinary fame and honor attached to martyrdom."[8] Some martyrs, like Ignatius, were showered with adulations before their martyrdom. Not that Ignatius sought martyrdom for personal praise, but he illustrates that it could be a temptation to some to seek to be immortalized in the annals of church history as a martyr for Christ. It was said of Polycarp, who was burned alive, that his bones were "more valuable than precious stones and finer than refined gold" and his grave became a sacred place to gather.[9] Recognizing the potential for such adulation, Paul finds it necessary to say that offering up one's life apart from love is a worthless sacrifice, an empty religious show, a hollow performance.

When it is motivated by the welfare of others and the glory of Christ, however, martyrdom becomes the ultimate sacrifice of love. Jonathan Edwards, in his book *Charity and Its Fruits,* summarizes God's perspective on love and self-sacrifice this way:

> [God] delights in little things when they spring from sincere love to himself. A cup of cold water given to a disciple in sincere love is worth more in God's sight than all one's goods given to feed the poor, yea, than the wealth of a kingdom given away, or a body offered up in the flames, without love.[10]

Only when martyrdom is the result of love for God and others is it the "more excellent way."

Divine Mathematics

Imagine for a moment what the Corinthians must have thought when they first heard Paul's words read publicly in the congregational meeting. They probably couldn't believe their ears! Paul's message was contrary to their entire way of thinking and behaving. They were deficient in love and they didn't even realize it! Their pride of knowledge and miraculous gifts had deceived them.

D. A. Carson, Bible commentator and professor of New Testament at Trinity Evangelical Divinity School, describes Paul's reasoning in this passage in terms of "divine mathematics." According to divine mathematics, "five minus one equals zero."[11] Or, as George Sweeting remarks, "gifts, minus love, equals zero."[12]

Author Jerry Bridges, giving a vivid illustration of divine mathematics, asks his readers to do this:

> Write down, either in your imagination or on a sheet of paper, a row of zeros. Keep adding zeros until you have filled a whole line on the page. What do they add up to? Exactly nothing! Even if you were to write a thousand of them, they would still be nothing. But put a positive number in front of them and immediately they have value. This is the way it is with our gifts and faith and zeal. They are the zeros on

the page. Without love, they count for nothing. But put love in front of them and immediately they have value. And just as the number two gives more value to a row of zeros than the number one does, so more and more love can add exponentially greater value to our gifts.[13]

Without love, our most extraordinary gifts and highest achievements are ultimately fruitless to the church and before God. In Paul's way of thinking, nothing has lasting spiritual value unless it springs from love.

A Modern Paraphrase

Picturing himself as the most extraordinary teacher or leader to ever live, Paul would say:

If I were the most gifted communicator to ever preach,
so that millions of people were moved by my oratory,
but didn't have love, I would be an annoying, empty wind-bag
before God and people.

If I had the most charismatic personality, so that
everyone was drawn to me like a powerful magnet, but
didn't have Christlike love, I would be a phony, a dud.

If I were the greatest visionary leader the church has ever heard,
but didn't have love, I would be misguided and lost.

If I were the bestselling author on theology and church growth,
but didn't have love, I would be an empty-headed failure.

If I sacrificially gave all my waking hours to discipling
future leaders, but did it without love,
I would be a false guide and model.

Notes to Chapter 1

1. William R. Moody, *The Life of Dwight L. Moody* (Chicago: Revell, 1900), 140. Also see Dwight Lyman Moody, *New Sermons, Addresses and Prayers* (Chicago: Goodspeed, 1877), 178.

2. Moody, *The Life of Dwight L. Moody,* 139.

3. Richard Ellsworth Day, *Bush Aglow: The Life Story of Dwight Lyman Moody, Commoner of Northfield* (Philadelphia: The Judson Press, 1936), 146; see also D. L. Moody, *Pleasure and Profit in Bible Study* (Chicago: The Bible Institute Colportage Association, 1895), 87.

4. Gregory J. Lockwood, *1 Corinthians*, Concordia Commentary (St. Louis: Concordia, 2000), 458.

5. John Short, "The First Epistle to the Corinthians," in *The Interpreter's Bible,* ed. Arthur C. Buttrick (New York: Abingdon-Cokesbury, 1953), 10:170.

6. George Sweeting, *Love Is the Greatest* (Chicago: Moody Press, 1974), 40.

7. George Muller was the founder and director of the Ashley Down Orphanage in Bristol, England; 122,683 orphans passed through this orphanage. Many biographies have been written on Muller's life of faith and prayer.

8. Rodney Stark, *The Rise of Christianity* (San Francisco: HarperCollins, 1996), 182.

9. *Martyrdom of S. Polycarp,* 18.

10. Jonathan Edwards, *Charity and Its Fruits* (1852; reprint ed., Edinburgh: Banner of Truth, 1978), 61-62.

11. D. A. Carson, *Showing the Spirit: A Theological Exposition of 1 Corinthians 12–14* (Grand Rapids, Mich.: Baker, 1987), 60.

12. Sweeting, *Love Is the Greatest,* 117.

13. Jerry Bridges, *Growing Your Faith* (Colorado Springs: NavPress, 2004), 164-65.

Chapter 2

Love or Die

But I have this against you, that you have abandoned the love you had at first.
Rev. 2:4

My own life-changing experience with love came when a friend gave me a copy of the book *Brother Indeed,* the biography of Robert C. Chapman from Barnstaple, England.[1] Apart from the Bible, no one has influenced my thinking about love and leadership more than Robert Chapman.

In his day, some called him an "apostle of love," and Charles Haddon Spurgeon referred to him as "the saintliest man I ever knew."

Robert Chapman left his profession as a lawyer in London to become pastor of a small Particular Baptist church in Barnstaple. This contentious little congregation had gone through three different pastors in the eighteen months prior to Chapman's arrival. The story of how Chapman completely turned around this fighting church by his love, patience, and Bible teaching ministry is an inspiring account of loving leadership. The church eventually became a large, harmonious church. It was known throughout England for its love, missionary outreach, and compassionate ministries to the poor.

By the end of his life, at age ninety-nine, Chapman had become so well known for his loving disposition and wisdom that a letter from abroad addressed simply to "R. C. Chapman, University of Love, England," was correctly delivered to his home.

Before Chapman arrived, the church in Barnstaple was proud of its doctrinal distinctives and church polity, but it was dying of lovelessness.

When Robert Chapman came, he breathed the life-breath of love into the church. It soon radiated with love for Christ, love for one another, love for the truth of the gospel, and love for the lost. It became a university of love.

In Revelation 2, we read of another church that was proud of its rightness and faithfulness, but was about ready to die for lack of love. Our Lord himself tells the church and its leaders to repent and allow the life-breath of love to flow back into its body. Read carefully the solemn words and warning of Jesus Christ to the church at Ephesus:

> I know your works, your toil and your patient endurance, and how you cannot bear with those who are evil, but have tested those who call themselves apostles and are not, and found them to be false.... But I have this against you, that you have abandoned the love you had at first. Remember therefore from where you have fallen; repent, and do the works you did at first. If not, I will come to you and remove your lampstand from its place, unless you repent. (Rev. 2:1-2, 4-5)

Commendation and Condemnation

Our Lord begins by commending the church of Ephesus for its good deeds, hard work, steadfastness in the faith, intolerance of heresy, zeal for doctrinal purity, and patient endurance under persecution. There is much to commend in this church, and we should prize its exemplary qualities. It would seem that all was well. The Ephesians could have written a book on successful church ministry. However, all was not well. Something was fundamentally wrong. With divine penetrating insight into the true spiritual state of this outwardly successful church, Jesus Christ turned from commendation to condemnation. He says, "But I have this against you, that you have abandoned the love you had at first."

In light of all the commendable qualities of this church, Christ's criticism might seem trivial. But in His eyes, the very inner heartbeat of the church's life was lost.

In light of all the commendable qualities of this church, Christ's criticism might seem trivial. But in his eyes, the very heartbeat of the church's life was lost.

Loss of First Love

At one time the church thrived with genuine love. But this had changed. There was still some measure of love left because they fought for the truth of the gospel and did good works (Rev. 2:2-3, 6). But their love was not what it once was. Indeed, instead of growing stronger and deeper as it should, their love had waned. They had works, but the joy, creativity, responsiveness, and energy that love produces had disappeared. The quality of their love had changed, and this became apparent even in their works. Jesus rebukes them and calls them to "do the works you did at first." He admonishes them to remember from where they "have fallen" (Rev. 2:5).

> **An earnest love makes us willing to give up our lives for one another.**

The object of this love is not specifically stated in the text. It does not say love for Christ or love for fellow believers. So it is best to understand Jesus to mean love in general (love for Christ, one another, and the lost).

The kind of love required by God of His people is total, undivided love (Deut. 6:4-6). We are to love God with *all* our heart and soul and mind (Matt. 22:37). Furthermore, according to the book of Revelation, the relationship between Jesus Christ and his church is that of a marriage relationship; Christ is the bridegroom and the church is the bride.[2] The response of the bride, the church, is to be joyous, undivided devotion to Christ the bridegroom. At Ephesus, the bride had lost important qualities of her love. The joy to worship, the hunger to know him better through his word, the desire to understand his love more fully, the thirst to grow spiritually, and the love of singing his praises and praying was lost.

The kind of love required among believers is to love one another as Jesus loved us. It is an earnest love (1 Peter 1:22) that makes us willing to give up our lives for one another (1 John 3:16). At Ephesus, the Lord was looking for his people to be sacrificially caring for one another's needs, opening their homes to one another, living like an extended family, joyously serving one another, praying fervently for one another, crossing racial boundaries, and enjoying life together in the church and home. But their love had withered away.

Amy Carmichael, who rescued abused children and provided a home for them through her Dohnavur Fellowship in India, recognized the deadly potential of loss of love among her coworkers. She laid down guidelines for the Sisters of the Common Life, the women who worked together with her in the orphanage:

> Unlove is deadly. It is a cancer. It may kill slowly but it always kills in the end. Let us fear it, fear to give room to it as we should fear to nurse a cobra. It is deadlier than any cobra. And just as one minute drop of the almost invisible cobra venom spreads swiftly all over the body of one into whom it has been injected, so one drop of the gall of unlove in my heart or yours, however unseen, has a terrible power of spreading all through our Family, for we are one body—we are parts of one another.
>
> We owe it to the younger ones to teach them the truth that united prayer is impossible, unless there be loyal love. If unlove be discovered anywhere, stop everything and put it right, if possible at once.[3]

The kind of love required by Christ is love for all people (1 Thess. 3:12). This love seeks to meet peoples' physical and spiritual needs. It is the love displayed by the Good Samaritan to an unknown dying man (Luke 10:30-37). It is the love expressed in evangelism and reaching out to the lost. It is the love Paul felt for Israel: "I have great sorrow and unceasing anguish in my heart. For I could wish that I myself were accursed and cut off from Christ for the sake of my brothers, my kinsmen according to the flesh" (Rom. 9:2-3). This love for the lost and the needy had shriveled away to nothing at Ephesus.

Tragically, the church at Ephesus had changed. It had abandoned its first love, and something had to be done or the Lord would judge his church. "No wonder," writes Puritan preacher Nathaniel Vincent, "that Satan, who labors to destroy churches, endeavors to kill love."[4]

Christ's Remedy for Diminished Love

Jesus calls upon the church to do three things immediately or, he says, "I will come and remove your lampstand." Although the exact meaning of this judgment is debated, the seriousness of the situation is alarmingly clear. Unless there is a change, Christ will come and will act in judgment against this local church.

Loss of love is sin. In Revelation 2:4-5 Jesus both rebukes and offers a remedy:

1. remember therefore from where you have fallen
2. repent
3. do the works you did at first

The situation was not past repairing, but the church had to take immediate action to rekindle the original flame of love. Failure to act would spell disaster for the church. The Lord ominously warns, "If not, I will come to you and remove your lampstand from its place, unless you repent." This warning demonstrates how seriously Jesus takes loss of love. He threatens that if they do not repent, he will come and remove their lampstand out of its place. That is, he will bring the existence of the local church to an end.

A Wake-up Call to All Churches and Leaders

The letters to the seven churches trumpet Christ's wake-up call to all churches and Christian leaders (Revelation 2–3). Jesus warns the local church at Ephesus and its leaders that they can work hard, fight heresy, have spiritual gifts, teach sound doctrine, and yet be deficient in love and on the verge of divine discipline. Since love is absolutely essential to the survival of the local church, its leaders must guard their own heartfelt love for Christ and continually monitor and encourage the church's love.

Guarding One's Own Love for Christ

When the leaders lose their love, it will not be very long before the people do. So leaders must first guard their own love relationship with the Lord Jesus Christ in order to protect the church from loss of love. There is no substitute for wholehearted, growing love for the Lord Jesus Christ. It is our first and most fundamental duty. The Ephesian believers thought their doctrinal orthodoxy was sufficient. But it was not. If we do not actively protect and cultivate our love for God and Christ,

"No wonder that Satan, who labors to destroy churches, endeavors to kill love."
—Nathaniel Vincent

all other loves wane: Our love for fellow Christians, our love for the needy, our love for the lost, and our love for the truth.

The Christian apologist Francis Schaeffer, who, with his wife Edith, modeled Christian love in remarkable ways through their open home in Switzerland, understood the importance of love:

> We must ask, *Do I fight merely for doctrinal faithfulness?* This is like the wife who never sleeps with anybody else but never shows love to her own husband. Is that a sufficient relationship in marriage? No, ten thousand times no. Yet if I am a Christian who speaks and acts for doctrinal faithfulness but do not show love to my divine bridegroom, I am in the same place as such a wife. What God wants from us is not only doctrinal faithfulness, but our love day by day. Not in theory, mind you, but in practice.[5]

C. H. Mackintosh, whose books on the Pentateuch are considered the standard for devotional commentaries, relates sound advice regarding love for Christ as the essential requirement:

> If I allow my work to get between my heart and the Master, it will be little worth. We can only effectually serve Christ as we are enjoying Him. It is while the heart dwells upon His powerful attractions that the hands perform the most acceptable service to His name.... True, he may preach a sermon, deliver a lecture, utter prayers, write a book, and go through the entire routine of outward service, and yet not minister Christ. The man who will present Christ to others must be occupied with Christ for himself.[6]

Love for God and Christ is foundational to a proper love for everything else. Love for God is the "great and first commandment" (Matt. 22:38).

Guarding against Externalism and Ritualism

We need to protect the church against the tendency to trust in external forms, religious rituals, traditions, and rules, while we neglect the vital elements of true love for Christ and one another.

The Ephesian believers, you can be sure, attended church, knew their doctrine, rejected false teachers, did good deeds, lived upright lives, prayed and sang, but the inner zeal and devotion of their love was dwindling to nothing. External performance had replaced true, inner, heart faith and love. The love for Christ and neighbor that they once had was gone. Thus their religion became more external than internal. It became more mechanical than heartfelt:

> They still proclaim the truth, but no longer passionately love him who is the truth. They still perform good deeds, but no longer out of love, brotherhood, and compassion. They preserve the truth and witness courageously, but forget that love is the great witness to truth. It is not so much that their genuine virtues have squeezed love out, but that no amount of good works, wisdom, and discernment in matters of church discipline, patient endurance in hardship, hatred of sin, or disciplined doctrine, can ever make up for lovelessness.[7]

Leading the Church in Repentance and Renewal

In a sin-saturated world, repentance and spiritual revitalization are never-ending tasks. So let the leaders and teachers of the church be prepared to lead the congregation in repentance for lovelessness and hypocritical love (Rom. 12:9). Love can be revived and grow afresh (Rev. 2:5). The fire can be rekindled. Lives can be rededicated to Christ and one another. The fresh life of love can be breathed into prayer, Bible study, evangelism, worship, and fellowship with others. To that end let us continually pray and work. As Puritan preacher Nathaniel Vincent prayed:

> O love! How much want is there of you in the Church of Christ! And how much does the Church feel for this want! It groans, it languishes, it dies daily because of your absence. Return, O love, return! Repair breaches, restore paths to dwell in, edify the old ways and places, and raise up the foundations of many generations.[8]

Notes to Chapter 2

1. Frank Holmes, *Brother Indeed: The Life of Robert Cleaver Chapman* (London: Victory Press, 1956). Holmes's biography is out of print. For a new biography see, Robert L. Peterson, *Robert Chapman* (Littleton, Colo.: Lewis & Roth, 1995). For a short summary of Chapman's life and some of the remarkable ways he dealt with people, see Robert L. Peterson and Alexander Strauch, *Agape Leadership: Lessons in Spiritual Leadership from the Life of R. C. Chapman* (Littleton, Colo.: Lewis & Roth, 1991).

2. Rev. 19:7, 9; 21:9; 22:17.

3. Frank Houghton, *Amy Carmichael of Dohnavur: The Story of a Lover and Her Beloved* (1979; reprint ed., Fort Washington, Pa., Christian Literature Crusade, 1992), 219.

4. Nathaniel Vincent, *A Discourse Concerning Love* (1684; reprint ed., Morgan, Pa: Soli Deo Gloria, 1998), 94.

5. Francis Schaeffer, *The Church before the Watching World* (Downers Grove, Ill.: InterVarsity, 1971), 60.

6. C. H. Mackintosh, *Genesis to Deuteronomy: Notes on the Pentateuch* (Neptune, NJ: Loizeaux, 1972), 155.

7. D. A. Carson, "A Church that Does All the Right Things, but …" *Christianity Today* (June 29, 1979): 30.

8. Vincent, *A Discourse Concerning Love*, 88.

Chapter 3

The Motivating Power
of Love

The love of Christ controls us.
2 Cor. 5:14

What motivates you to want to lead and teach people? Desire to help people, a sense of duty, enjoyment of leadership, money, the pleasure of teaching people, peer pressure? For Christian leaders, the primary answer must be love. Love is the greatest motivating power in the universe. It is at the heart of the gospel. God's love moved him to give his Son for our salvation. Love is the indispensable motivating force for all Christian service. Leadership is to be motivated by a threefold love: Christ's love for us, our love for Christ and love for others.

Motivated by the Love of Christ

In a profoundly revealing passage of Scripture, Paul discloses the single, driving, motivating force of his life:

> For the love of Christ controls us, because we have concluded this: that one has died for all, therefore all have died; and he died for all, that those who live might no longer live for themselves but for him who for their sake died and was raised. (2 Cor. 5:14-15)

Please note that Paul is not speaking about his love for Christ, but about Christ's love for him. Paul never ceased to be amazed by Christ's love for sinners as demonstrated by his death on the cross. Christ's love totally controlled his life. It is the reason for all that Paul did.

One missionary who understood Paul's grasp of the love of Christ wrote, "If Jesus Christ be God and died for me, then no sacrifice can be too great for me to make for Him."[1] Hymn writer Isaac Watts captured Paul's understanding of this love in the lyrics to *When I Survey the Wondrous Cross*. The hymn ends with the unforgettable line, "Love so amazing, so divine, demands my soul, my life, my all."

> **"Love so amazing, so divine, demands my soul, my life, my all."**
>
> **—Isaac Watts**

Understanding the love of Christ is so essential to Christian living that Paul, in one of the most magnificent prayers in the Bible, prays that God would empower all believers to grasp the vast, incomprehensible nature of the love of Christ:

> that you … may have strength to comprehend with all the saints what is the breadth and length and height and depth, and to know the love of Christ that surpasses knowledge. (Eph. 3:17-19)

Although it "surpasses knowledge," the love of Christ is something we are to grasp not only intellectually but experientially, personally, and intimately. Biblical commentator Harold Hoehner highlights this paradox:

> The very fact that Christ's love expressed itself in his willingness to die on behalf of sinners is in itself beyond one's comprehension. The reality of Christ's love is overwhelming to all believers.... No matter how much knowledge we have of Christ and his work, his love surpasses that knowledge. The more we know of his love, the more we are amazed by it.[2]

History provides many examples of leaders and teachers who tell of the motivating power of the love of Christ. Methodist preacher and pastor William Alfred Quayle, for example, recorded a conversation he had with a horseback-riding, frontier preacher to the North American settlers during the 1800s. The pioneering missionary said to Quayle,

I feel the woes of the heathen: I know the bitter barrenness of their lives; but this would not suffice to keep me among them. One gets used to heathenism and grows callous to its desperate tragedy. Not the love of man sufficeth to keep me away from my wife and from my children through these years. Only the love of Christ is competent.[3]

Iain Murray tells us it was the realization of Christ's love that influenced renowned preacher D. Martyn Lloyd-Jones to leave his prestigious medical career to preach God's Word:

he came to see the love of God expressed in the death of Christ in a way which overwhelmed him. Everything which was happening to him in his new spiritual life was occurring because of what had first happened to Christ.[4]

Hope MacDonald, missionary to Brazil, describes her realization of God's love:

I saw for the first time the ancient truth, "We love him, because he first loved us" (1 John 4:19 KJV). How had I overlooked it? I had memorized that verse before I started school! As the reality of His love *for me* engulfed me for the first time, I wanted to get out of bed and jump for joy. I wanted to climb to the top of the roof and shout to the world, "Wake up! God loves me!" It was a moment I will never forget. Since then I have never doubted His love for me.[5]

And Hudson Taylor, founder of the China Inland Mission (now called the Overseas Missionary Fellowship) believed that if money could motivate the merchants of England to cross life-threatening oceans and enter the interior of China at great personal risk of loss of life, could not the love of Christ motivate missionaries to do the same for the sake of the gospel?[6]

The great truth we must come to again and again throughout life is this: Not that we love God, but that he first loved us and demonstrated his love by sending "his only Son into the world ... to be the propitiation for our sins" (1 John 4:9-10). This is what should most thrill our hearts and motivate us to serve others.

Motivated by Love for Christ

Knowing Christ and grasping his great love compels us to serve him, but even more, it causes us to love him. We love him because he first loved us (1 John 4:19), and he gives us the ability to love others. Love is to be our chief motivation for serving people. It is to be the sustaining power that enables us to endure the many difficulties of leadership.

Our Lord says the "great and first commandment" is to love God with the totality of our being—"with all your heart and with all your soul and with all your mind" (Matt. 22:35-40).

> There is hardly anything better we can do for those we lead than to love the Lord Jesus Christ supremely and keep our love relationship with him fresh and growing every day!

Jesus Christ is to be the supreme object of our affections. More than anything or anyone else in the world he is to be loved, treasured, and enjoyed. He is to be loved above all other people, even our closest family members: "Whoever loves father or mother more than me is not worthy of me, and whoever loves son or daughter more than me is not worthy of me" (Matt. 10:37).

When our leadership is motivated by love for God and Christ, we are most pleasing to God and most effective with people. You may be a highly skilled public speaker and a dynamic leader, but if you don't love God first and foremost, you will not be pleasing to him. Your leadership will not be godly or Spirit-empowered leadership. Ministry for ministry's sake does not please God; rather, it is ministry born of love for him that is pleasing and acceptable (1 Cor. 13:1-3). "All the commandments," writes David Jones, "are to be performed out of love for him, even the service of neighbor as well as the service of worship."[7]

We should, of course, seek to continually improve our skills in leadership, personal discipline, time management, interpersonal relationships, and teaching. But above all these things, we should seek to increase our knowledge and enjoyment of Christ and deepen our love for him (Phil. 3:8-14). After all, the deeper our love for him the more we will become like him in love and the more we will be able to teach others to love.

There is, therefore, hardly anything better we can do for those we lead than to love the Lord Jesus Christ supremely and keep our love relationship with him fresh and growing every day! Out of this blessed and holy love relationship will come a greater manifestation of God's love in us, shining out to others and drawing them to Christ.

Amy Carmichael lived such a life of love:

> the love of God within her was so powerful a magnet that all through her life others were drawn irresistibly to her. It was little wonder that the Hindus began to call her "the child-catching Missie Ammal," and they truly believed that she used some mysterious powder which drugged their children and made them long to be near her.[8]

Caring for the Lord's people is not always a pleasant experience. The very people we pour our lives out to serve are imperfect and sinful. They can turn on us and attack maliciously. They can be unreasonable, demanding, and ungrateful.

Two of the most godly leaders ever to have graced this world were Moses and David, yet at times people complained bitterly about them and even were ready to kill them. It is no different for leaders of God's people today. An elder in a church told me how he had experienced numerous abuses during the many years he had served his local church. He had been physically choked,

> If money could motivate the merchants of England to cross life-threatening oceans and enter the interior of China at great personal risk of the loss of life, could not the love of Christ motivate the missionaries to do the same for the sake of the gospel?

punched, had his jaw broken, been spit on, cursed at, falsely accused, and threatened with a lawsuit.

This kind of abusive treatment by people helps explain why so many pastors and church workers become bitter and disillusioned with people and leave the work of the Lord. But when our service is motivated by love for Christ, we will be better able to persevere and find greater fulfillment in our labors. Oswald Chambers, author of the classic devotional *My Utmost for His Highest*, said it well:

> The work of feeding and tending sheep is hard work, arduous work, and love for the sheep alone will not do it; you must have a consuming love for the Great Shepherd, the Lord Jesus Christ. Then He will flow through you in a passion of love and draw men to Himself.[9]

Here, then, is a key to endurance in spiritual leadership: We must serve people out of love for Christ. When we do, we will have joy in the work, and, most important, our service will be acceptable and pleasing to God. Being motivated, therefore, by the love of Christ and love for Christ is essential to Christian leadership. It is the starting point for all Christian service.

Motivated by Love for People

Hours before his death, after washing their feet, Jesus gave his disciples "a new commandment":

> A new commandment I give to you, that you love one another: just as I have loved you, you also are to love one another. By this all people will know that you are my disciples, if you have love for one another. (John 13:34-35)

One simply cannot understand Christian living, evangelism, or church leadership without grasping the new commandment. Note that Jesus didn't merely say "love one another." He said something far more profound: Love one another "just as I have loved you." Jesus sets his own example of love. His love is a love for the unlovely as well as the lovely. It is a caring, serving love. It gives itself unselfishly for the good of others. That is why he gave us the example of washing the disciples' feet and of sacrificing his life on the cross. He was establishing a new pattern of love.

John explains the full implication of imitating Jesus' love when he writes, "By this we know love, that he laid down his life for us, and we ought to lay down our lives for the brothers" (1 John 3:16). Benjamin B. Warfield says, "Self-sacrificing love is thus made the essence of the Christian life."[10]

The new commandment applies to every Christian, and especially to leaders and teachers. All of our work—leading, teaching, correcting, protecting, speaking, serving, motivating, organizing, planning, visiting, praying, counseling, or evangelizing—is to be shaped by the new commandment. We are to love others as Jesus loved. We are to love as the Good Shepherd who laid down his life for the sheep (John 10:11).

More than any other leader in the New Testament, Paul displayed Jesus' self-sacrificing love for those he taught and led. Paul's handling of the turbulent church at Corinth illustrates his love-motivated leadership. The church at Corinth caused Paul much heartache. Most of us would have given up and walked away in anger, yet despite the grief they caused him, Paul repeatedly affirmed his love for them.

Commentator Paul Barnett remarks, "Historically, few ministers can have suffered at the hands of their congregations as much as Paul had from the behavior of the Corinthians. Yet he continued to hold them in his heart."[11]

In 2 Corinthians Paul says, "I said before that you are in our hearts, to die together and to live together" (2 Cor. 7:3). Later in the same letter he writes, "I seek not what is yours but you.... I will most gladly spend and be spent for your souls" (2 Cor. 12:14-15). James Denny refers to this as "one of the most movingly tender passages in the whole Bible."[12] Denny goes on to say, "'Not yours, but you' is the motto of every minister who has learned of Christ."[13]

From his extensive study of 2 Corinthians, which reveals Paul's heart and life, Philip Hughes writes, "No man on earth had a warmer and more devoted heart than the Apostle Paul. Love was the impulse of his whole life and ministry as Christ's Apostle."[14]

Paul had enormous giftedness, but it was his love that allowed him to "endure all things" (1 Cor. 13:7) and deal effectively with troubled people. It is no different for Christian leaders and teachers today. Consider, for example, Anthony Norris Groves, a missionary to Iraq and India. He has been called the "Father of Faith Missions." Like Paul, he

> "Self-sacrificing love is thus made the essence of the Christian life."
> —B. B. Warfield

suffered much for Christ. Yet one of the shining qualities of his life was his selfless love for people. This love was rooted in his love for Christ.

Biographer Robert Dann noted how Groves' love for people made him a great missionary despite his weaknesses:

He was not a gifted evangelist, nor a natural orator. He was not particularly sociable, and he often found relationships painful. He was never a great organiser or administrator; he was not physically or mentally tough.... One might think he was not cut out to be a missionary at all. But he had one quality that more than made up for his deficiencies: he knew how to love. Love was the key to everything: "I feel there is something in love so *hallowing*; it kills that hateful selfishness which twines round all that is human." It was love that drew people to Christ—not ceremonies or rules or customs, or even doctrines, but love. And it was love that drew people to Norris Groves.[15]

John Christian Arulappan, an Indian evangelist and church planter who saw thousands converted and many churches established in India, also affirms Groves' influence of love. He writes: "He loved me sincerely as his dear child in Christ Jesus. I never knew anyone who loved me so for the sake of the Lord Jesus."[16]

Love motivated leadership will make an impact because people are hungry for love. This point was brought home to me by two friends who planted a church. Soon after the church had been established, they organized a question and answer session for the new congregation. During the meeting, a young lady who had recently become a Christian asked them this question: "Would you be willing to die for me?"

Her question caught them completely off guard. Not wanting to be glib, they gave her a wise response. They told her they first needed to examine their own hearts honestly before God to see if they really loved her that much. After they had done that, they would answer her. This young convert's question was a thoroughly biblical question. How would you have answered her?

Notes to Chapter 3

1. Norman Grubb, *C. T. Studd: Cricketer and Pioneer* (Fort Washington, Pa.: Christian Literature Crusade, 1933), 132.

2. Harold W. Hoehner, *Ephesians: An Exegetical Commentary* (Grand Rapids: Baker, 2002), 489-90.

3. William A. Quayle, *The Pastor-Preacher*, ed. Warren W. Wiersbe (Grand Rapids, Mich.: Baker, 1979), 39.

4. Iain H. Murray, *David Martyn Lloyd-Jones: The First Forty Years 1899-1939* (Edinburgh: Banner of Truth, 1982), 85.

5. Hope MacDonald, *Discovering the Joy of Obedience* (Grand Rapids, Mich.: Zondervan, 1971), 45.

6. A. J. Broomhall, *Hudson Taylor and China's Open Century*, vol. 3: *If I Had a Thousand Lives* (London: Hodder and Stoughton, 1982), 442.

7. David Jones, "Love: The Impelling Motive of the Christian Life," *Presbyterion* 12 (Fall 1986): 65.

8. Frank L. Houghton, *Amy Carmichael of Dohnavur* (1979; reprint ed., Fort Washington, Pa.: Christian Literature Crusade, 1992), 105.

9. Oswald Chambers, *The Complete Works of Oswald Chambers* (Grand Rapids, Mich.: Discovery, 2000), 1361.

10. Benjamin Breckenridge Warfield, "The Emotional Life of Our Lord," in *The Person and Work of Christ* (Philadelphia: Presbyterian and Reformed, 1950), 64.

11. Paul Barnett, *The Second Epistle to the Corinthians*, NICNT (Grand Rapids, Mich.: Eerdmans, 1997), 361.

12. James Denny, *The Second Epistle to the Corinthians,* The Expositor's Bible (New York: Funk & Wagnalls, 1900), 363.

13. Ibid., 365.

14. Philip Edgcumbe Hughes, *Paul's Second Epistle to the Corinthians*, NICNT (Grand Rapids, Mich.: Eerdmans, 1962), 390.

15. Robert Bernard Dann, *Father of Faith Missions: The Life and Times of Anthony Norris Groves* (Waynesboro, Ga.: Authentic Media, 2004), 372.

16. Ibid., 372.

Part Two

The Character and Behavior
of a Loving Leader

Chapter 4

Patient and Kind

Love is patient and kind.
1 Cor. 13:4

Imagine more than three hundred Christians from forty different nations and various denominational backgrounds living together twenty-four hours a day. Imagine them working together in extremely tight quarters, most of them for two years, some for even longer. Imagine them doing all of this as unpaid volunteers! Such is life aboard the ship MV *Doulos*.

For the past twenty-seven years, the *Doulos* has sailed around the world stopping at ports in more than a hundred countries and serving as a Christian book exhibit and conference center visited by eighteen million people. The *Doulos,* and two other similar ships, are the result of the vision of George Verwer, founder of Operation Mobilization (known as OM).[1] OM was one of the first, short-term mission organizations and has trained more than 150,000 people in missions.

The volunteers who serve on the ship are ordinary people. They have the same weaknesses and character flaws as other human beings. They experience aboard the *Doulos* the same difficulties people experience ashore. The only difference is that on the ship there is no running away from conflict. How can they live and work together under such extreme conditions without destroying one another? The answer: love.

From the very start of OM, George Verwer preached that without a "revolution of love"[2] the vision for the ships and for the thousands of short-term literature teams would be an impossible dream. The kind of love necessary for working together on these ships is not a sentimental, fluffy love.

It is Calvary's selfless, self-sacrificing love. It is the kind of love described in 1 Corinthians 13:4-7: love that is patient and kind, love that does not envy or boast, is not arrogant or rude, does not insist on its own way, and is not irritable or resentful. It is Christlike love.

Instructions, Not Poetry

First Corinthians 13 is not a theoretical discourse on love or a flowery hymn glorifying the feelings of love. Paul was not a romantic poet. He was an apostle of Jesus Christ—a global missionary, church planter, pastor, and teacher. These words are a critical part of his instruction and correction to the church at Corinth, which was being torn apart by loveless behavior.

In order to help the Corinthians understand their own deficiencies and the "more excellent way," Paul lists fifteen positive and negative descriptions of love. In the Greek text, all of these descriptions are verbs describing what love does and doesn't do. In English, these descriptions are often translated as adjectives.

Love is
 1. patient
 2. kind

Love is *not*
 3. envious
 4. boastful
 5. arrogant
 6. rude
 7. selfish
 8. easily angered
 9. resentful
10. joyful over wrongdoing

Love
11. rejoices with the truth
12. bears all things

13. believes all things
14. hopes all things
15. endures all things

These fifteen qualities beautifully portray the character and behavior of the Lord Jesus Christ. We are to pattern our love and leadership after him (1 John 2:6). With Christ living and working within us through the Holy Spirit, the same behaviors should be true of us—whether we are elders, pastors, deacons, youth workers, Sunday school teachers, music directors, missionaries, evangelists, Bible study leaders, or church administrators.

In our ministry with people, these qualities should be uppermost in our mind. One of the most important chapters in the Bible for life in the local church and for Christian leadership is 1 Corinthians 13. It defines how we should behave in marriage, friendship, church, and society. It describes what our character should be like—and *in Christian ministry, character is everything.*

Paul didn't just write pretty words about love, he lived them, and the Corinthians saw the truth of these words in his life.

Love Is Patient

If we were to ask our Lord, "What is a loving Christian leader like?" he would first answer, "patient and kind." So Paul begins and ends his love catalog with the patient, enduring nature of love (1 Cor. 13:4, 7). In an imperfect world, a leader must be characterized by patience.

The Greek verb for patience denotes "longsuffering" or "forbearance," particularly in respect to personal injuries or wrongs suffered. The Christian spirit of love does not seek to retaliate. It is not quick to anger.

God himself is the supreme example of longsuffering.[3] When we are tempted to be impatient with others, we should stop and think about the gracious longsuffering of God with us and our many wrongs against him. In light of his patience toward us, who are we to think that we cannot patiently bear with the weaknesses and failures of others—or the wrongs they may have done to us?

God himself is the supreme example of longsuffering.

Lack of patience is a serious deficiency in a Christian leader. Our work with people is primarily a spiritual work, so it must be done God's way, with great patience and care. An impatient leader is as destructive to people as an impatient father is to his children or as an impatient shepherd is to his sheep.

Patience is needed because life is full of frustrations, hurts, and injustices. In fact, it is impossible to lead people without eventually being attacked. People will assail their leaders' character, criticize their decisions, speak evil behind their backs, and take advantage of their love.

In response to such attacks, love suffers long. So Paul instructs the Lord's servant to be patient when wronged:

> And the Lord's servant must not be quarrelsome but kind to everyone, able to teach, patiently enduring evil, correcting his opponents with gentleness. God may perhaps grant them repentance leading to a knowledge of the truth, and they may escape from the snare of the devil, after being captured by him to do his will. (2 Tim. 2:24-26)

Also, patience is needed when dealing with people's many weaknesses and failures. We must have patience to bear with those who are slow to learn, resistant to change, weak in faith, quick to complain, forgetful of their responsibilities, emotionally unstable, fearful, or wayward. Paul teaches that we are to "admonish the idle, encourage the fainthearted, help the weak, *be patient with them all*" (1 Thess. 5:14). Also, Paul instructs Timothy: "preach the word ... reprove, rebuke, and exhort, *with complete patience*" (2 Tim. 4:2; italics added).

> **A lack of patience in a Christian leader is a serious deficiency. An impatient leader is as destructive to people as an impatient father is to his children or as an impatient shepherd is to his sheep.**

Patient Leaders in Action

Being patient doesn't imply passivity or a refusal to confront people's sins or problems. Without his patient pastoral leadership, Paul and the Corinthians would have gone their separate ways. Instead, his firm yet patient handling of the problems preserved the relationship. When the Corinthians unjustly criticized him, Paul didn't give up on them, cut them off, become vindictive, return evil for evil, or express anger in a sinful way. Instead, he answered their criticisms, confronted their sins, and warned of discipline. What is even more remarkable is that he did so with true patience and heartfelt love.

Paul, therefore, could say to the Corinthians that his leadership was marked by patience, kindness, and love:

We put no obstacle in anyone's way, so that no fault may be found with our ministry, but as servants of God we commend ourselves in every way ... [by] patience, kindness, the Holy Spirit, genuine love. (2 Cor. 6:3-4, 6)

Patience is just as important in church leadership today as it was in Paul's day. Many times a leader's patience is put to the test. Robert Chapman, for example, was well known for his love. And like all loving leaders, he showed remarkable patience with difficult people and problems.

Perhaps his patience and love was most evident when a clash developed in a prominent church in Plymouth, England, between two powerful personalities: John Nelson Darby, the architect of dispensational theology, and Benjamin W. Newton, the primary teacher of the church. When Darby and Newton were unable to reconcile their differences, Darby announced plans to start a new, rival church in Plymouth. Darby's proposal alarmed many people within the church, as well as those who attended churches associated with it. Because of Robert Chapman's love for both men, he felt compelled to seek reconciliation. He urged Darby not to proceed with his intentions, but Darby refused to heed Chapman's advice.

Darby's action created two similar congregations in Plymouth of about equal size. These churches continued to be at odds with each other, which caused other churches of similar beliefs to choose sides. Then, a year later, John Darby made more serious accusations against B. W. Newton's doctrine. In time, Newton recognized his doctrinal error and publicly confessed his wrong. But Darby and his colleagues insisted that Newton's reversal was not genuine. Over time they were able to influence many other churches to exclude Newton and his church from their circle. Newton recognized defeat and left the church in Plymouth permanently, but the battle was far from over. It would escalate beyond all reasonable proportion, as church fights often do, causing untold heartache. People on both sides were heart-broken over the bitter division and made continued attempts at reconcili-ation, but to no avail. A meeting of twelve influential leaders convened to try to resolve the growing divisions. During the meeting, Robert Chapman made one of his most memorable statements. He challenged John Darby: "You should have waited longer before separating," referring to Darby's in-ability to resolve his conflict with B. W. Newton.

"I waited six months," Darby replied.

Chapman's reply was uncharacteristically testy: "But if it had been at Barnstaple, we should have waited six years."

History proved Darby to be impatient and harsh—not only with B. W. Newton but with many others.[4] Although some began to speak of Darby in less than gracious terms and refuse him fellowship, Robert Chapman did not. His love for John Darby remained unabated. Instead of disparaging Christian brothers and sisters who followed Darby, he referred to them as "brethren dearly beloved and longed for." Chapman's sorrow was genuine because he lived according to the "more excellent way."

Love Is Kind

Paul's first two descriptions of love are paired together and balance each other perfectly: Love suffers long (the passive quality) and love shows kind-ness (the active quality). Patience and kindness are two sides of the same coin of love. "You can no more have love without kindness than you can have springtime without flowers," writes W. Graham Scroggie.[8]

Kindness is a readiness to do good, to help, to relieve burdens, to be useful, to serve, to be tender, and to be sympathetic to others. It has been said, "Kindness is love in work clothes."

God is kind to all,[6] and the work of our Lord Jesus Christ on earth demonstrated abundant and compassionate kindness. The gospels are re-plete with stories of his kindness to needy men and women: Jesus touched a man, whom Luke the physician described as "full of leprosy" (Luke 5: 12-13). William Lane accurately describes this as "an unheard-of act of compassion."[7] When Jesus encountered a deformed woman bent over by disease and a demonic agent, "he laid his hands upon her" (Luke 13:13). He touched the eyes of the blind and fed the multitudes. He made time to stop and bless little children. Jesus ate and talked with the most hated people of his day, the tax collectors. A notoriously immoral woman found kindness and mercy at his feet (Luke 7:37-39). Acts 10:38 sums up the work of Jesus this way: "He went about doing good."

The Power of Kindness

Scripture insists that all those who lead and teach the Lord's people are servants who must be kind to everyone (2 Tim. 2:24). "As servants of God," Paul writes, "we commend ourselves in every way" by patience and kindness (2 Cor. 6:4, 6).

Augustine, in his book *Confessions,* describes how even during his unconverted days, the renowned preacher and bishop, Ambrose, moved him more by kindness than even by excellent preaching:

> That "man of God" received me like a father and expressed pleasure at my coming with a kindness most fitting in a bishop. I began to like him, at first indeed not as a teacher of the truth, for I had absolutely no confidence in your Church, but as a human being who was kind to me.[8]

Loving leaders are kind, even to people who criticize, antagonize, or oppose them. It was said of Thomas Cranmer, an archbishop of the Church of England: "To do him any wrong was to beget a kindness from him."[9]

Leadership without kindness is a disaster. The Old Testament account of King Rehoboam, Solomon's son, for example, illustrates how unkindness ruined a king. Before Rehoboam was coronated, the people of Israel came to him and demanded to know the spirit in which he would rule them because his father's rule ended in harsh oppression. Before answering the people, he rightly consulted with the elders—experienced men who had served his father and knew good and bad leadership principles. They counseled Rehoboam to lead with a kindly disposition. They said, "If you will be good [kind] to this people and please them and speak good words to them, then they will be your servants forever" (2 Chron. 10:7).

Disregarding the wisdom and experience of these older men, Rehoboam rejected their counsel. He foolishly chose the counsel of his young, inexperienced friends to treat the people with a harsh, heavy hand (2 Chron.

10:10-11). As a result, the nation divided in civil war. The people wanted a kind king, not a harsh one. And people are no different today. Kindness is a key to leading people effectively.

If we want to reach and influence people for Jesus Christ, we must cultivate a kindly disposition. Acts of kindness impact people in big ways and capture their attention: a card sent to one who is sick, a concerned phone call, an invitation to dinner, a readiness to help relieve a burden, a caring voice, a gentle touch, a thoughtful gesture, a simple expression of interest in another's concerns, a visit. The way of kindness is the "more excellent way."

> **If we want to reach and influence people for Jesus Christ, we must cultivate a kindly disposition.**

Notes to Chapter 4

1. The other ships are the MV *Logos* (1970–88), which sank off the coast of Chili, and the MV *Logos II* (sailing since 1990). A newly acquired ship is *Logos Hope,* which will replace *Logos II.* To read the thrilling stories of two of these ships see Elaine Rhoton, *The Doulos Story* (Carlisle, England: OM Pub., 1998) and Elaine Rhoton, *The Logos Story* (Waynesboro, Ga.: OM Lit., 1988).

2. George Verwer, *The Revolution of Love* (Waynesboro, Ga.: OM Lit., 1993).

3. Ex. 34:6; Isa. 7:13; Jer. 15:15; Rom. 2:4; 9:22; Gal. 5:22; 1 Tim. 1:16; 2 Peter 3:9, 15.

4. Jonathan D. Burnham, *A Story of Conflict: The Controversial Relationship between Benjamin Wills Newton and John Nelson Darby* (Waynesboro, Ga.: Paternoster Press/Authentic Media, 2004).

5. W. Graham Scroggie, *The Love Life: A Study of 1 Corinthians 13* (London: Pickering & Inglis, n.d.), 39.

6. Ruth 2:20; 2 Sam. 9:3; Ps. 106:7; 145:17; Luke 6:35; Rom. 2:4; 11:22; Eph. 2:7; Titus 3:4; 1 Peter 2:3.

7. William L. Lane, *The Gospel According to Mark,* NICNT (Grand Rapids, Mich.: Eerdmans, 1974), 87.

8. Augustine, *Confessions,* trans. Henry Chadwick (Oxford: Oxford University Press, 1992), 88.

9. Alfred Tennyson, *Queen Mary* (Boston: James R. Osgood, 1875), 194.

Chapter 5

Not Envious or Boastful

Love does not envy or boast.
1 Cor. 13:4

On Paul's second missionary journey he traveled to the city of Corinth, where he stayed for eighteen months (Acts 18:11). Corinth at the time was a prosperous Roman colony, and Paul viewed it as a strategic city for the advancement of the gospel. It was a miniature Rome, a booming, wealthy commercial center. Corinth could offer its citizens and travelers all the pleasures of a free-minded, cosmopolitan city. People in that culture valued success through wealth, personal status seeking, competitive individualism, wisdom, and knowledge. This value system not only permeated the culture but also adversely influenced the church. According to one commentator, "The problem was not that the church was in Corinth but that too much of Corinth was in the church."[1]

When Paul wrote 1 Corinthians some three and a half years after leaving that city, he had to address serious problems within the congregation. At the root of these problems were the worldly attitudes and beliefs that were inherently hostile to the gospel of the cross of Christ and its wisdom.

As a result of numerous sins in the church, Paul is compelled to take a negative tack, describing eight character qualities that are inconsistent with love. These eight qualities—all betraying a sinful lack of love—divided the church at Corinth just as they divide churches today.

Paul plainly states that love is *not*

1. envious
2. boastful

3. arrogant
4. rude
5. selfish
6. easily angered
7. unforgiving
8. joyful over wrongdoing

These eight vices are totally incompatible with love. In brief, they express the self-centered life that tears apart relationships and spoils the unity that should characterize every local church. Paul's list serves as an objective standard to correct our selfish behaviors and to guide us on the "more excellent way."

Love Does Not Envy

Topping Paul's list is a vice that has wrecked countless relationships and split many churches—envy or jealousy. Jealousy divided the church at Corinth, and it belied the Corinthians' empty boast of being spiritual people: "For while there is jealousy

Envy is totally incompatible with love.
It destroys love, and with it a leader's character.

and strife among you, are you not of the flesh and behaving only in a human way?" (1 Cor. 3:3).

Envy makes one resentful of others' good fortune. It covets others' gifts, possessions, or positions of influence. It is suspicious and critical of another's popularity. Nathaniel Vincent pointedly expresses the tormenting, selfish spirit of envy:

> How much of hell is there in the temper of an envious man! The happiness of another is his misery, the good of another is his affliction. He looks upon the virtue of another with an evil eye, and is as sorry at the praise of another as if that praise were taken away from himself. Envy makes him a hater of his neighbor, and his own tormentor.[2]

Envy is totally incompatible with love. It destroys love—and with it, a leader's character.

Envy Is Destructive

The account of King Saul and David provides a vivid illustration of the destructive power of envy in a leader's life. Initially Saul loved David, but almost immediately after the shepherd boy's stunning victory over the giant Goliath, the king became envious of him.

There was much to envy about David. He was young, handsome, strong, brilliant, talented, and popular. A successful warrior, he was abundantly blessed by God in all that he did, and "his name was highly esteemed" (1 Sam. 18:30). He was so popular and greatly admired that the women sang, "Saul has struck down his thousands, and David his ten thousands" (1 Sam. 18:7).

This comparison of Saul's victories with David's greater achievements enraged the king and stirred up the vilest passions of jealousy. He came to hate David and opposed him at every turn. He spoke evil against him at every opportunity and thought only of David's downfall. Rather than repent of his envy and seek God's help in acknowledging David as God's gift to the nation, Saul gave full vent to his sin. His envy led to discontentment, paranoid thinking, personal misery, and murderous scheming. In the end, Saul destroyed himself and lost his kingdom. His life proved that where there is envy and jealousy there is not love.

None of us are immune from petty, self-centered envy. Even the most committed missionaries and servants of the Lord have struggled with this sin. George Muller was the founder of the Ashley Down orphanage in Bristol, England. While co-pastoring with Henry Craik at a church in Bristol, England, George Muller saw that people enjoyed the other man's teaching more than his own. Henry Craik was not only an excellent Bible teacher, but he was also a first rate classical and Hebrew scholar. Unlike King Saul, however, Muller was a man of extraordinary faith and prayer. He confessed his envious feelings toward his co-worker and confronted his sin:

> When in the year 1832, I saw how some preferred my beloved friend's ministry to my own, I determined, in the strength of God, to rejoice in this, instead of envying him. I said, with John the Baptist, "A man can receive nothing, except it be given him from heaven" (John 3:27). This resisting the devil hindered separation of heart.[3]

George Muller's and Henry Craik's friendship lasted for thirty-six years, until Craik died.[4] Although both were strong, multi-gifted men with quite different personalities, their long relationship was a public testimony to the power of Christian love. Muller was well known for his many lifelong friendships with people like Hudson Taylor, Charles Spurgeon, D. L. Moody, Robert Chapman, and others. Envious people, unfortunately, have few real friends and many conflicts.

We need to be aware that envy is a prevalent sin among the Lord's people and Christian leaders. Pastors can go to bizarre extremes to eliminate from the church gifted people who threaten them. Churches can envy other churches that are larger or are growing rapidly. Missionaries can envy other missionaries who are more fruitful or better supported. Bible study leaders can envy more popular Bible study leaders; singers can envy other singers who sing more often or receive louder applause; elders can envy fellow elders who shine brighter in leadership ability or knowledge; and deacons can envy fellow deacons who serve more effectively or are sought out for help more frequently.

Love Rejoices in Others

Love "does not burn with envy."[5] Love is large-hearted, other-oriented, content, and full of good will toward others. "When love sees someone who is popular, successful, beautiful, or talented, it is glad for them and never jealous or envious."[6] Brotherly love tries to "outdo one another in showing honor" (Rom. 12:10).

The loving Barnabas, Paul's co-worker, for example, rejoiced over Paul's greater giftedness and invited him into significant ministry opportunities as a colaborer teaching in the church at Antioch (Acts 11:19-26). The loving Jonathan, King Saul's son, differed greatly from his envious father. He admired and valued David's leadership abilities. He was willing to jeopardize his own future role as a king (1 Sam. 23:16-17) in order to protect and promote David's cause.

As Christian leaders, our commitment to love should prompt us to consciously rejoice over the successes and talents of others. We should seek to advance the ministry opportunities available to others and treat their strengths and gifts as if they were our own (1 Cor. 12:25-26). When feelings of envy toward others arise, we must confess those feelings for what they are—sin and self-centeredness. Like George Muller, we must be determined, in the strength of God, to rejoice in the other person's success. We will be happier and more content and God will be pleased when we think and act according to the "more excellent way."

Love Does Not Boast

Like the sin of envy, boasting, or bragging, is a sinful preoccupation with oneself. Braggarts crave attention. They want others to praise their abilities, knowledge, successes, and even their sufferings for God. Because they desire recognition, they speak too highly and too much of themselves, although they may have nothing significant to say.

Boasting has long been a serious problem among religious people. The sanctimonious, trumpet-blowing Pharisees shamelessly craved the attention of people. They were religious show-offs. Jesus pointed out how they loved the front seats in the synagogue, respectful greetings on the street, and praise for their public acts of piety. Likewise, believers in the church at Corinth boasted about their superior wisdom, their favorite teacher's speaking skills, and their extraordinary spiritual experiences. They were full of themselves, not full of love.

Such boasting is still a problem today. I clearly remember a missionary evangelist who came to my home, along with others, for dinner. For three hours he never stopped talking about himself, his ministries, and his success. He told us how hard he worked, how far and wide he traveled, and how blessed he was of God. Not once, however, during the long evening meal did he inquire about others at the table. He was a boaster.

Another time I was at a church conference that had hundreds of book and ministry exhibits. Our book table was next to a ministry booth featuring an internationally known pastor and author. The entire time he was at his booth he talked nonstop about himself. We couldn't help but overhear him praise himself for two full days. He told every person he talked to how large his church was, how many people were on his staff, and how large the church budget was. He wasn't even subtle about dropping the names of the famous people he knew and places he had preached. He was a braggart.

Boasting, however, helps no one. We speak of "empty boasting," but in fact, as Scroggie says, "There is no other kind of boasting. The very nature and essence of a boast is emptiness. Boasting is always an advertisement of poverty."[7] Boasting does not build up or serve the church community. Boasting does not honor Christ. Rather, it intimidates and it divides people. It provokes others to envy. Boasting is particularly abhorrent in a leader. It mars a leader's character. We wouldn't want people in the church to follow such an example. Braggarts blatantly disregard God's prohibition against self-praise: "Let another praise you, and not your own mouth; a stranger, and not your own lips" (Prov. 27:2).

Braggarts build themselves up, jealous people tear others down, but loving people build others up.

Love Promotes and Praises Others

Love promotes and praises others. It is self-effacing and shies away from speaking of itself. So those who are possessed of Christ's love delight in focusing attention on others, in pushing others to center stage, and in sharing the spotlight of attention.

In the context of thinking about spiritual giftedness, Paul writes, "I say to everyone among you not to think of himself more highly than he ought to think, but to think with sober judgment" (Rom. 12:3). This doesn't imply that we never talk about ourselves or allow others to inquire about our interests or ministries. There's a fine line between speaking about ourselves in a nonboastful way and boasting in a sinful, self-centered way. Like Paul and Barnabas, missionaries need to report on God's work through their labors to those who support them (Acts 14:27; 15:3). Skillful teachers often use illustrations taken from their personal experiences to communicate effectively

> **Braggarts build themselves up, jealous people tear others down, but only loving people build others up.**

without boasting (Gal. 2:1-14). The difference is that braggarts use people to fulfill their own need for attention and praise.

A missionary friend on the way back to Africa found himself on board a ship with the young Billy Graham and witnessed love that does not brag. Graham was on his way to the London Crusade. As the two men met and talked together during their voyage, something about Graham touched my friend deeply. Graham asked questions about my friend's life and ministry in Africa; he was genuinely interested in his work. My friend particularly

observed that Graham rarely spoke about himself or his phenomenal experiences as an evangelist. At the end of their voyage, the missionary asked
the young evangelist how he could pray for
him, and the answer was, "Pray that I will be
a humble man." That prayer many years ago
reflected a heart of wisdom and love. Decades
later it is apparent that pride of gift or success
is not a criticism that has been leveled against Billy Graham.

> **"Boasting is always an advertisement of poverty."**
> —W. Graham Scroggie

There is something to learn from his example. *Humble people are not self-absorbed braggarts.* Instead, they promote and praise others according to the "more excellent way" of love.

Notes to Chapter 5

1. David E. Garland, *1 Corinthians*, BECNT (Grand Rapids, Mich.: Baker, 2003), 8.
2. Nathaniel Vincent, *A Discourse Concerning Love* (1684; reprint ed., Morgan, Pa.: Soli Deo Gloria, 1998), 82.
3. W. Elfe Tayler, *Passages from the Diary and Letters of Henry Craik of Bristol* (London: Paternoster, n.d.), xiii.
4. His biographer notes:

> No feature of Mr. Craik's character was more conspicuous than that of love. It beamed forth in his countenance, it betrayed itself in the very tones of his voice, and his life was a practical comment on that word, "Do good to all." Hence his earnestness of manner in preaching; hence his acute sensibility in contemplating the prospects of humanity; hence his intense sympathy with the sorrows of others, and his extreme affection towards his friends, and especially the members of his family. Surely a more loving, sympathizing spirit has rarely left this world.

Tayler, *Passages from the Diary and Letters of Henry Craik of Bristol,* 307.
5. Anthony C. Thiselton, *The First Epistle to the Corinthians*, NIGTC (Grand Rapids, Mich.: Eerdmans, 2000), 1048.
6. John MacArthur, *1 Corinthians* (Chicago: Moody Press, 1984), 340.
7. W. Graham Scroggie, *The Love Life: A Study of 1 Corinthians 13* (London: Pickering & Inglis, n.d.), 40.

Chapter 6

Not Arrogant or Rude

Love ... is not arrogant or rude.
1 Cor. 13:4-5

Hardly anything is more contrary to the example of Christ, the message of the cross, and Christian love than arrogant self-importance. Christians are sinners saved by God's grace, and all of our spiritual gifts and ministries have been graciously given to us by God. Thus the Scripture says, "What do you have that you did not receive? If then you received it, why do you boast as if you did not receive it?" (1 Cor. 4:7).

There is no place whatsoever for egotism in the Lord's work, especially for those who lead and teach the community of the cross. Yet arrogance is a widely recognized problem among leaders today.

During a seminary graduation ceremony I attended, the president of the seminary delivered a challenging message entitled "Big-Shot Syndrome." It was gratifying to hear him warn the graduating students against thinking too highly of themselves and acting like big shots rather than humble servants of Jesus Christ. To bring his point home, he had cut a towel into small squares and put them in a basket. At the end of his message he invited the graduates to come forward to receive a small piece of towel. He then suggested that they place the piece of towel in their wallets to continually remind them that Jesus Christ took a towel and humbly washed his disciples' feet. What an excellent reminder to those young servants of the gospel. Remembering Christ's example of humility is good for anyone who serves in local church leadership.

Love Is Not Arrogant

An arrogant spirit permeated the church at Corinth, and this generated many of its problems.[1] Arrogance is contrary to love because it focuses on self more than others. Arrogant people, especially religious ones, think they are better than other people. They think they know a lot more than they actually do, they consider themselves holier than others, and they imagine themselves more gifted than they really are. They are blind to their own glaring sins, personal weaknesses, and doctrinal errors. As Amy Carmichael once said, "Those who think too much of themselves don't think enough."[2]

> "Nothing sets a Christian so much out of the devil's reach than humility."
> —Jonathan Edwards

The Greek word for *arrogant* can be literally rendered "puffed up" or "inflated." J. B. Phillips captures the idea well in his translation: Love does not "cherish inflated ideas of its own importance."[3] In other words, love doesn't have a superiority complex. This was an important concept for Jesus' disciples to understand because many of the religious leaders of their day were puffed up with religious pride. One self-inflated Pharisee was observed praying to himself: "God, I thank you that I am not like other men" (Luke 18:11).

In contrast, Jesus strictly prohibited his disciples from any kind of idolatrous self-exaltation: "The greatest among you shall be your servant. Whoever exalts himself will be humbled, and whoever humbles himself will be exalted" (Matt. 23:11-12). Humility of mind, not arrogance, is to be the badge of Christ's followers. Arrogance is the disposition of the devil (Isa. 14:13-14), not of Christ. And, as Jonathan Edwards wisely observed, "Nothing sets a Christian so much out of the devil's reach than humility."[4]

A New Testament example of an arrogant, big-shot church leader is Diotrephes. The Bible says he loved to be "first." John writes:

> I have written something to the church, but Diotrephes, who likes to put himself first, does not acknowledge our authority. So if I come, I will bring up what he is doing, talking wicked nonsense against us. And not content with that, he refuses to welcome the brothers, and also stops those who want to and puts them out of the church. (3 John 9-10)

Diotrephes was so puffed up with himself he criticized and refused to listen to the beloved apostle John. He abused people who disagreed with him, created an atmosphere of fear within the local church, and demanded his own way. He was not a builder of people but a limiter of people. He was not a uniter but a divider. He was not a humble-minded servant leader. He would not share the ministry with peers and colleagues such as Paul. He refused godly correction and instruction. His heart was not contrite before God, and his arrogant spirit divided people and hurt the church. In Paul's words, Diotrephes was "a noisy gong or a clanging cymbal" (1 Cor. 13:1).

Love Is Humble and Modest

The nature of love is the opposite of arrogance. Love thinks humbly and modestly about self and others (Rom. 12:3). The spirit of love says, "Do not be haughty, but associate with the lowly. Never be conceited" (Rom. 12:16). Peter exhorted the church elders to "Clothe yourselves, all of you, with humility" (1 Peter 5:5). Paul reminded the Ephesian elders that he served "the Lord with all humility" (Acts 20:19).

Humility is the mindset of a servant. It makes a leader more teachable, more receptive to constructive criticism, better able to work with others, better qualified to deal with other people's failures and sins, more willing to submit to others, less prone to fight, and quicker to reconcile differences. Without humility, one cannot be a Christlike leader (Matt. 11:29; Phil. 2: 7-8).

Humility also makes teachers of the Word better able to relate to people at all levels of life, even the poorest and least educated, as did our Lord Jesus Christ. Teachers of God's Word must be humble servants or they contradict the message of the Bible.

Paul and Apollos were highly gifted leaders and teachers. They could easily have been tempted to be puffed up with feelings of superiority because of their brilliant minds and many successes in the gospel. Yet Paul wisely reminds the Corinthians, who prized big-shot teachers, that he and Apollos were humble servants of the Lord, nothing more. He writes, "What then is Apollos? What is Paul? Servants through whom you believed, as the Lord assigned to each [of us]" (1 Cor. 3:5).

Loving leaders and teachers, then, are humble and modest. They do not treat people arrogantly, but respectfully. They humbly serve and lift up others, not themselves.

C. S. Lewis, one of the world's best-known Christian authors, was a humble man who as a teacher lived out the "more excellent way" of love. Lewis taught at Oxford and Cambridge Universities in England and became internationally famous when he converted from atheism to Christianity. He wrote many Christian books that have sold in the millions and been translated into many languages. His writings have touched countless lives for Jesus Christ.

Despite enormous worldwide success, Lewis was a humble man and a teacher of both scholars and children, and available to all kinds of people who sought his advice. He personally answered thousands of letters from ordinary people he had never met but who asked for his help. Lewis believed God wanted him to answer every letter, which he did, and "he treated each correspondent as if he or she were as important as the king or queen of England."[5] This is a remarkable accomplishment given his demanding schedule. He answered people's questions about depression, marital conflict, and difficult theological problems. He also committed himself to praying daily for many troubled people worldwide who requested his prayers—people he never met and some who were quite eccentric.

Lewis (an Anglican) attended the local Anglican church near his home, where he related to a diverse group of people, some of whom had little realization of his literary success or worldwide popularity. Since heaven would be filled with all kinds of people worshiping God, Lewis considered it "unthinkable" to seek a church with a membership made up only of academic and scholarly types. Worshiping at his local church was, for him, preparation for heavenly worship.[6]

His humble attitude toward others is revealed in a delightful story told by his taxi driver, Clifford Morris (Lewis didn't own a car). Lewis treated him, as he did everyone, with caring and attentive respect. One of C. S. Lewis's biographers, Lyle W. Dorsett, writes:

> [Morris] found Mr. Lewis to be warm and congenial, always treating him as an equal despite the wide disparity between their social classes and educational levels. This treatment surprised and blessed Morris, because other men—including Christians—were never so generous.

Occasionally, Professor Lewis would get into the car and on the way to Cambridge say, "Morris, I'm sorry I can't talk for a quarter of an hour. I need to do my prayers."[7]

C. S. Lewis keenly understood the necessity of humility for Christian living and the many dangers of sinful pride. Of pride he wrote, "It was through Pride that the devil became the devil: Pride leads to every other vice: it is the completely anti-God state of mind."[8]

Those who live by the "more excellent way," however, don't suffer from an "anti-God state of mind." Instead, like their Savior, they are "gentle and lowly in heart" (Matt. 11:29).

Love Is Not Rude

Christlike love is to influence all behaviors, and Scripture tells us that love is not rude; it does not "behave with ill-mannered impropriety."[9] The verb for "rude" conveys the idea of acting disgracefully, contrary to established standards of proper conduct and decency. Thus inappropriate dress, inconsiderate talk, disregard for other people's time or moral conscience, taking advantage of people, tactlessness, ignoring the contributions and ideas of others, running roughshod over other's plans and interests, inappropriate behavior with the opposite sex, basic discourtesy and rudeness, and a general disregard for proper social conduct are all evidence of a lack of love and have no place in the local church.

A lack of love was evident in the rude behavior of the church at Corinth. Richer members didn't wait for poorer ones to arrive for the Lord's Supper. Instead, they selfishly ate their own expensive foods and left little food for the poor to eat (1 Cor. 11:21-22, 33).

Other members thoughtlessly used their so-called superior knowledge and liberties to trample over the consciences of their weaker brothers and sisters. They ate foods offered to pagan idols (1 Cor. 8), which created confusion and caused some believers to violate their conscience. During congregational meetings, certain gifted speakers were monopolizing the time and hindering others from expressing their spiritual gifts. Then there were those who interrupted while others were speaking. Some spoke in tongues without interpretation so the people didn't know what was being said. To put an end to their ill-mannered impropriety, Paul instructed that "all things should be done decently and in order" (1 Cor. 14:40).

Rudeness did not die out with the church in Corinth but characterizes our day as well. During a worship service in a church I was visiting, two young people in back of me were disgracefully disrupting the celebration of the Lord's Supper. They crunched on nuts and hard candies. They gulped water from plastic bottles, and every time they took a drink, the plastic water bottle popped. They whispered to one another and said "amen" along with the congregation, but only in mockery. They disturbed everyone around them.

After the service, I spoke to one of the church leaders about their behavior. He sighed in frustration. He assured me that they had tried to address the problem on other occasions, but that the parents refused correction. They felt their children had a right to eat and drink during the service. Of course, this kind of behavior isn't allowed in a movie theatre, but the parents thought it acceptable in church. They were rude, unloving people who had no regard for others.

Rudeness is not limited to age or social class. Intellectuals and highly educated people can be just as rude and thoughtless as anyone. At a Christian university, a conservative scholar presented a lecture on an unpopular, politically incorrect subject. As he spoke, the audience of scholars and leaders booed, hissed, and laughed at the speaker. This disgraceful display of rudeness with no regard for the speaker's feelings or beliefs was a far cry from love. Love is not rude.

Love Promotes Proper Decorum

Loving people are considerate of how their behavior affects others, even in little things. Those who are possessed of God's love are sensitive to proper social relationships, public decency, social convention, politeness, tact, and proper conduct in dress, speech, and action.

We must resist the acceptance of rude behavior.

They are sensitive to the fact that people in certain churches would be upset if a preacher or song leader didn't wear a tie and jacket but wore jeans and a sweatshirt. They recognize that it would be inappropriate for a female Sunday school teacher to come to class dressed in clothes appropriate for the beach (1 Tim. 2:9-10). They would know better than to talk on a cell phone during a public church meeting.

Love recognizes that ill-mannered, rude behavior disrupts elder and deacon meetings (and all other committee meetings). Love fosters effective meetings in which all things are done properly and in an orderly fashion (1 Cor. 14:40). Talking over people, not listening, ignoring other people's ideas, making cutting comments and threats, bullying, and showing disrespect to those who disagree does not exemplify love. Such behavior has no place in church leadership.

As Western societies become more coarse and thoughtless of basic standards of courtesy and social decency, we must resist the acceptance of rude behavior. If not, it will have a harmful, degrading effect on our lives and on our churches.

This is an especially important issue to Christians who travel to other countries for Jesus Christ. Hudson Taylor was one of the greatest Christian leaders of all times, and he was acknowledged to be a loving leader. The remarkable story of his life and the founding of the China Inland Mission has been extensively documented.[10] One of Taylor's many leadership strengths was

> "In nothing do we fail more, as a Mission, than in lack of tact and politeness."
> —Hudson Taylor

his ability to relate well to the Chinese because of his keen sense of propriety and his cultural sensitivity. At one time he complained in a letter about the lack of tact and—in effect, disrespect—some missionaries displayed toward Chinese customs and protocol, which are an important element of Chinese culture. His words should be heeded today:

> Some persons seem really clever in doing the right thing in the worst possible way, or at the most unfortunate time. Really dull, or rude persons will seldom be out of hot water in China; and though earnest and clever and pious will not effect much. In nothing do we fail more, as a Mission, than in lack of tact and politeness.[11]

Christ's Great Commission (Matt. 28:18-20) has given all Christians a global mission. Paul recognized this. A man of three different cultures—Jewish, Roman, and Greek—Paul, the evangelist, traveled extensively for the gospel and knew how to adapt properly to various social mores (1 Cor. 9:19-23; 10:32-33). We also, when we travel for Christ, need to be sensitive not to offend the societal conventions of our host nation but to be good ambassadors of God's love to all people.

Following the more excellent way of love means being keenly aware of what is considered tactful and polite in other cultures and being respectful of different people's social customs.

Notes to Chapter 6

1. The verb for "arrogant," *phusioō*, appears seven times in the New Testament, six of those in 1 Corinthians (4:6, 18-19; 5:2; 8:1; 13:4).
2. Quoted in Wayne A. Mack, *Humility: The Forgotten Virtue* (Phillipsburg, N.J.: P&R Publishing, 2005), 61.
3. J. B. Phillips, *The New Testament in Modern English,* rev. ed., (New York: Macmillan, 1972), 361.
4. Jonathan Edwards, "Undetected Spiritual Pride," http://www. bible teacher.org/ jedw_19.htm (accessed Sept. 19, 2005).
5. Lyle W. Dorsett, *Seeking the Secret Place: The Spiritual Formation of C. S. Lewis* (Grand Rapids, Mich.: Brazos Press, 2004), 118.
6. Dorsett, *Seeking the Secret Place*, 41.
7. Dorsett, *Seeking the Secret Place*, 42.
8. C. S. Lewis, *Mere Christianity* (San Francisco: HarperCollins, 2001), 122.
9. Anthony C. Thiselton, *The First Epistle to the Corinthians*, NIGTC (Grand Rapids, Mich.: Eerdmans, 2000), 1049.
10. See A. J. Broomhall, *Hudson Taylor & China's Open Century* 7 vols. (London: Hodder and Stoughton).
11. Broomhall, *Hudson Taylor & China's Open Century*, vol. 5: *Refiner's Fire* (London: Hodder and Stoughton, 1985), 231.

Chapter 7

Not Selfish or Easily Angered

Love ... does not insist on its own way; it is not irritable.
1 Cor. 13:5

The Bible doesn't hide the fact that even among the apostles, selfish attitudes and power struggles existed. James and John, for example, thinking exclusively of themselves, asked Jesus to give them places of highest honor in the kingdom: "Grant us to sit, one at your right hand and one at your left, in your glory" (Mark 10:37). James and John were "card-carrying members of the 'self-seekers' club."[1] Their request immediately sparked conflict among the other disciples, as selfish ambition always does. Mark records that "when the ten heard it, they began to be indignant at James and John." They became indignant because they, too, were self-seekers and craved positions of power and glory for themselves.

This incident shows how little they understood their Lord's ways and how much they had yet to learn about loving and serving one another as brothers. "James and John want to sit on thrones in power and glory," writes John Stott; "Jesus knows that he must hang on a cross in weakness and shame. The antithesis is total."[2]

Love Is Not Preoccupied with Self

The fifth negative statement aims at selfishness, the root of many of our problems, a vice totally incompatible with Christian love and leadership. Love, 1 Corinthians 13:5 states, "does not insist on its own way." This means

63

that love does not seek its own interests or its own advantage. Love "is not preoccupied with the interest of the self."[3] This is especially important to understand because we live in an age of radical individualism. People in many modern Western societies are consumed with their own self-interest. They place themselves at the center of the universe, which is the rightful place of God. This all-consuming focus on self is completely contrary to Christian love.

If Jesus had sought his own advantage there would have been no cross. But the Scripture says, "Christ did not please himself" (Rom. 15:3). Our Lord came not to be served but to serve: "I am among you as the one who serves" (Luke 22:27).

Paul, too, did not seek his own way. If he had, he would never have endured all the grief involved in spreading the gospel and caring for the churches. But because of his love for Christ, expressed through love for others, he could say, "I try to please everyone in everything I do, not seeking my own advantage, but that of many" (1 Cor. 10:33). "For though I am free from all, I have made myself a servant to all" (1 Cor. 9:19). "I seek not what is yours but you.... I will most gladly spend and be spent for your souls" (2 Cor. 12:14-15).

This was not an easy example for the Corinthian believers to follow. In stark contrast, they insisted on their rights and freedoms to eat foods offered to pagan idols, even if taking such liberties hurt the conscience of their weaker brothers and sisters (1 Cor. 8-10). They didn't understand the spirit of love that says, "If food makes my brother stumble, I will never eat meat, lest I make my brother stumble" (1 Cor. 8:13). It didn't matter to them that "if your brother is grieved by what you eat, you are no longer walking in love" (Rom. 14:15). They used their marvelous liberties and gifts for their own selfish ends rather than for the good of the whole community.

"Christ did not please himself."
Rom. 15:3

As self-seekers, they also didn't understand Christian ministry or the servant role of a Christian leader or teacher. Some at Corinth even viewed Paul's suffering and selfless life as an example of weakness and failure. Their view of Christian leadership was power and rulership, not weakness and servanthood; therefore, they doubted his apostleship. These same misconceptions about true Christian leadership persist today.

Love Is Occupied with Others

The great enemy of every shepherd is a selfish heart. A wonderful New Testament model of a loving leader and teacher is Barnabas. He was not a self-oriented throne seeker. Luke records that he was "a good man, full of the Holy Spirit and of faith" (Acts 11:24). Being full of the Holy Spirit, he was characterized by love (Gal. 5:22) and all the qualities of love described in 1 Corinthians 13:4-7.

> **Barnabas thought more of what was best for the new church than his own prominence and security.**

The first time we meet Barnabas in the New Testament he is selling land and giving the money to the poor saints in Jerusalem (Acts 4:36-37). Generosity toward others naturally flows out of love. As Robert Law says, "Love is the giving impulse."[4]

But what is most impressive about Barnabas is how he shared his leadership position and ministry with Paul. Barnabas had been sent by the leaders in Jerusalem to help with the newly established church in Antioch. It was an exciting place to be. God was doing new things among the Gentiles, and Barnabas was at the center of the action. Yet he thought more of what was best for the new church than his own prominence and security.

Believing that the church needed Paul's extraordinary giftedness, Barnabas traveled, at great personal sacrifice, to the city of Tarsus to find Paul and invite him to Antioch to teach. This meant Barnabas would be sharing his teaching and leadership role with Paul, who was far more gifted. Barnabas pushed Paul forward, and later Paul became the more prominent of the two. As one preacher aptly observed, "Barnabas was not a ministry hog." He didn't have to do all the ministering or get all the glory. Barnabas was not a throne seeker; he was a washer of feet (John 13:14). He was a lifter of people, not a limiter of people (Acts 11:19-24). He was a giver, not a taker. His love was the "giving variety," not the "getting variety."[5]

Barnabas was truly a loving Christian leader and teacher. He was not jealous of Paul, nor did he brag of his status as an apostle or of his own spirituality. He was not arrogant, rude, or selfish, but he gave himself for the benefit of others. No wonder the people called him "son of encouragement" (Acts 4:36; 11:23). He exemplified the motto: "Great things can happen when you don't care who gets the credit." Great things happened in the church at Antioch through Barnabas and Paul—and continue to happen in the church today—because of unselfish teachers and leaders.

A modern day Barnabas is John Stott, former rector of All Souls Church in London, honorary chaplain to the Queen of England, and author of many excellent biblical commentaries. A missions professor recounts that while walking through an airport, he saw an elderly man sitting in the airport chapel with a large pile of letters at his side, writing. It was John Stott. Like a loving shepherd, Stott wrote and encouraged many people, especially young people. And like Barnabas, John Stott is well known as a gracious servant of God who shared his teaching and leading ministry with others.[6]

Stott's lowly servant heart is illustrated by an account given by one of his Latin American colleagues who translated Spanish for him while he was speaking in Cuba:

> … after I finished five days of translating for [John Stott], he invited me to do some birdwatching with him but I fell very ill. What a privilege it was to be fed, cared for, prayed over, comforted and affectionately ministered to by him. I have the impression that the chambermaids in the hotel where we stayed thought that I must be an extremely important person because I was being taken care of by a distinguished white, Anglo-Saxon gentleman—something they had never seen before.[7]

Loving leaders and teachers—whether Sunday school teachers or missionary evangelists—unselfishly give their time, energy, and possessions to help people. They put themselves out to serve others, they reach out to people in need, they are self-forgetful and ultimately self-renouncing. They don't belong to themselves and they are not concerned about being unfairly treated; they are not worried about being repaid or even properly thanked. They are godly people who look not only to their own interests, but also to the interests of others (Phil. 2:4).

Love Is Not Easily Provoked

A remarkable quality of love is that it is not easily provoked to an emotional state of anger. "It is not irritable." This is an eminently practical virtue for a leader. Leaders have to deal with a lot of difficult situations. There will always be plenty of fuel to provoke a leader to anger, irritability, offense, bitterness, and resentment. This is why one of the biblical qualifications for an elder is that he not be "quick-tempered" (Titus 1:7). Shepherds can't be kicking or killing the sheep because they are upset.

This doesn't mean that one never gets angry or irritated with people. The Bible doesn't say love does not get angry; it says love is not easily provoked to anger or irritation. There is righteous, controlled anger motivated by love and opposed to evil and falsehood that senselessly destroys people.[8] But love is not provoked in a destructive sense

> **"The heart of man is exceedingly prone to undue and sinful anger, being naturally full of pride and selfishness."**
> **—Jonathan Edwards**

because of wrong motives. "The heart of man," says Jonathan Edwards, "is exceedingly prone to undue and sinful anger, being naturally full of pride and selfishness."[9] This anger is incompatible with love.

A seminary professor tells the story of being at a restaurant with a pastor when the server accidentally poured water over the pastor's suit. The pastor angrily snapped at the server, giving full vent to his displeasure. After cleaning up, the professor leaned over and whispered to the pastor, "Maybe we should witness to her of the love of Christ." The pastor got the message.

A loving heart (like Christ's) would immediately have felt compassion for the server and thought more of her feelings than of a soiled suit. It would have sought to ease the tension by downplaying the situation and reassuring the server. The incident could have easily been turned into a positive witness for Christ. Instead, the pastor thought only of himself and his suit. He was easily provoked.

Outside the church, such leaders misrepresent Christ and give his people a bad name in the world. And within the church, it is easy to see how those who are easily provoked to anger carelessly frighten, hurt, and divide people. They invite and accentuate conflict.

Angry people are focused not on others but on their own emotions and issues. When leaders are angry, problems are exaggerated, miscommunication and misunderstanding abound, and objectivity and reason disappear. When anger rules, small problems become big explosions that can blow a church to pieces. I am convinced that *much more damage is done to our churches by out-of-control anger than we care to admit.* It is a big problem.

The devil is a master at using anger to ruin churches and families, and he can often provoke godly leaders to do destructive things to others. None of us are immune from hurting people with our anger. Henry Drummond insightfully observes that anger is "the vice of the virtuous." Consider how quick we are to downplay and justify our angry outbursts toward others:

> We are inclined to look upon bad temper as a very harmless weakness.... And yet here, right in the heart of this analysis of love, it finds a place; and the Bible again and again returns to condemn it as one of the most destructive elements in human nature.
>
> *The peculiarity of ill temper is that it is the vice of the virtuous. It is often the one blot on an otherwise noble character.* You know men who are all but perfect, and women who would be entirely perfect, but for an easily ruffled, quick-tempered, or "touchy" disposition. The compatibility of ill temper with high moral character is one of the strangest and saddest problems of ethics[10] [italics added].

As Christians, when we face conflict and relational pain we are to be Spirit-controlled and self-controlled (Gal. 5:22-23). Out-of-control anger is the work of the flesh and the devil (Gal. 5:19-20; Eph. 4:30-32). There is an old saying that when you spill over a vase, what's inside is what comes out. When you are dealing with someone who is disagreeable or thoughtless, or who simply sees things differently than you do, what comes out of *you*? Take this matter seriously before the Lord and guard yourself from any self-justification.[11] The Scripture says, "Let every person be ... slow to anger; for the anger of man does not produce the righteousness that God requires" (James 1:19-20).

Love Is Calm and Slow to Anger

Loving leaders are not irritated by every little disagreement or frustration. The reason for this is that love, as we have already seen, is *patient.* Love suffers long with the wrongs inflicted by others. Those who control their anger control potentially explosive situations and bring healing to damaged emotions: "He who is slow to anger quiets contention" (Prov. 15:18).

Martyn Lloyd-Jones tells how Hudson Taylor was slow to anger and irritation. In China, standing at the bank of a large river, Hudson Taylor called for a riverboat to take him across the river. As the boat arrived at shore, a wealthy Chinese man came up behind Taylor in a hurry to get into the boat. The man pushed Hudson Taylor aside with such force that he fell into the mud. Horrified by what he had seen, the boatman refused to allow the wealthy man to board his boat because Taylor had been first to call for his services and was a foreigner who deserved, by Chinese customs, to be treated with respect. The rich man didn't realize Hudson Taylor was a foreigner because of his Chinese dress. When he realized what he had done, he instantly apologized. Hudson Taylor didn't react with irritation or anger; instead, he graciously invited the man to join him in the boat and witnessed to him of Christ's love.[12] He responded to a provoking situation according to the "more excellent way."

Notes to Chapter 7

1. Lewis B. Smedes, *Love Within Limits: Realizing Selfless Love in a Selfish World* (Grand Rapids, Mich.: Eerdmans, 1978), 42.

2. John Stott, *The Cross of Christ* (Downers Grove, Ill.: InterVarsity, 1986), 286.

3. Anthony C. Thiselton, *The First Epistle to the Corinthians*, NIGTC (Grand Rapids, Mich.: Eerdmans, 2000), 1050.

4. Robert Law, *The Tests of Life: A Study of the First Epistle of St. John* (Edinburgh: T&T Clark, 1914), 72.

5. I. Howard Marshall, *The Epistles of John*, NICNT (Grand Rapids, Mich.: Eerdmans, 1978), 126.

6. Timothy Dudley-Smith, *John Stott: A Global Ministry* (Leicester, England: InterVarsity, 2001), 21.

7. Ibid., 454.

8. Num. 16:15; Ps. 7:11; Nahum 1:2, 6; John 2:13-17; Eph. 4:26.

9. Jonathan Edwards, *Charity and Its Fruits* (1852; reprint ed., Edinburgh: Banner of Truth, 1978), 201.

10. Henry Drummond, *The Greatest Thing in the World* (1874, reprint ed., Burlington, Ont.: Inspirational Promotions, n.d.), 21-22.

11. Jonathan Edwards remarks, "Men are often [accustomed] to plead zeal for religion, and for duty, and for the honour of God, as the cause of their indignation, when it is only their own private interest that is concerned and affected.

It is remarkable how forward men are to appear, as if they were zealous for God and righteousness, in cases wherein their honour, or will, or interest has been touched, and to make pretence of this in injuring others or complaining of them" (Edwards, *Charity and Its Fruits*, 198).

12. D. Martyn Lloyd-Jones, *Studies in the Sermon on the Mount*, 2 vols. (Grand Rapids, Mich.: Eerdmans, 1971), 1:281-82.

Chapter 8

Not Resentful or Joyful
over Evil

Love is not resentful; it does not rejoice at wrongdoing,
but rejoices with the truth.
1 Cor. 13:5-6

Despite R. C. Chapman's loving character, there were people who despised him. A local grocer in the city of Barnstaple, for example, was so upset at Chapman's open-air preaching that once he spit on him! For a number of years, the grocer continued to criticize and publicly interrupt Chapman's open-air preaching. Chapman continued on in his ministry and, when the opportunity presented itself, reached out to bless the grocer.

The opportunity came when one of Mr. Chapman's wealthy relatives came to visit him. The visit was more than just a social call. The relative wanted to see Chapman's ministry of hospitality and outreach to the city's poor. After an informative visit, the relative asked if he could buy groceries for the ministry. Mr. Chapman gladly agreed, but he insisted that the groceries be purchased at a certain grocer's shop—the one who had for so long vehemently maligned him.

Unaware of previous interactions between the grocer and Chapman, the relative went where he had been directed. He selected and paid for a large amount of food, then told the grocer to deliver it to Robert Chapman. The stunned grocer told the visitor that he must have come to the wrong shop, but the visitor explained that Chapman had sent him specifically to that shop. Soon the grocer arrived at Mr. Chapman's house, where he broke down in tears and asked for forgiveness. That very day, the grocer yielded his life to Christ!

"To forgive without upbraiding, even by manner or look," wrote Robert Chapman, "is a high exercise of grace—it is imitation of Christ."[1]

Love Does Not Hold Grudges or Seek Revenge

Another lofty, redeeming quality of love is that it is not resentful. The literal translation is love "does not reckon the evil." Commentator David Garland explains the imagery conveyed by these words: "Love does not keep books on evil.... The image is of keeping records of wrongs with a view to paying back injury."[2] Love does not hold grudges or seek revenge. It does not keep "a private file of personal grievances that can be consulted and nursed whenever there is possibility of some new slight."[3]

Jay Adams, a Christian counselor and author of numerous books on counseling, relates the story of a troubled couple who visited a Christian counselor for help. The wife's physician had advised her to see a counselor because she was developing an ulcer that apparently had no physical cause. During the session, the wife slammed down on the counselor's desk a manuscript "one-inch thick, on 8½ by 11 paper, typewritten on both sides ... a thirteen–year record of wrongs that her husband had done to her."[4]

If we enjoy nursing old wounds, we will be devoured by bitterness.

The counselor could immediately see that the wife's resentment of her husband's many faults and her meticulous documentation of each one had made her bitter. Keeping a record of her husband's sins had only made matters worse, to the point of causing this woman to become physically ill. So the counselor wisely reminded her of 1 Corinthians 13, emphasizing this: Love does not keep records of all the wrongs one has suffered at the hands of others.

The freedom not to keep records of wrongs suffered is vital to love. We all have been hurt by evil inflicted on us by others. We all have had to struggle with forgiveness. We all have had to let go of bad memories and give up any desire for revenge in order to be reconciled with those who have injured us. There is no way we could live happily together in marriage or with other believers in the local church without this quality of love. If we refuse to let go of emotional hurts, if we enjoy nursing old wounds, if we feel compelled to get even with our enemies, we will be devoured by bitterness, anger, and unforgiveness. We will be miserable examples and ineffective leaders for Christ.

Love Forgives

All the outstanding men and women of God through the ages have suffered terrible injustice and criticism, yet they have taken the opportunity to become forgiving people rather than resentful people. There is never an excuse for returning evil for evil or for destroying another person's life (Rom. 12:21). Being hurt is actually an opportunity to practice the "new commandment," to walk the royal road of love, to feed and care for your enemy, to "heap burning coals on his head," to "overcome evil with good" (Rom. 12:14, 19-21). It is an opportunity to suffer for the Lord's sake and to imitate God's forgiving love: "[Forgive] one another, as God in Christ forgave you ... be imitators of God, as beloved children. And walk in love, as Christ loved us and gave himself up for us" (Eph. 4:32–5:2).

What a mighty power is love that can overcome evil, cover painful memories, forgive, forgo revenge, and arrest resentment. Love, Lewis Smedes writes,

> does not have to clear up all misunderstandings. In its power, the details of the past become irrelevant.... Accounts may go unsettled; differences remain unsolved; ledgers stay unbalanced. Conflict between people's memories of how things happened are not cleared up; the past stays muddled.... Love prefers to tuck all the loose ends of past rights and wrongs in the bosom of forgiveness—and pushes us into a new start.... [Moving] toward a reconciled life is one of the hardest things any human being is ever asked to do. Love is the power to do that.[5]

To choose the path of love doesn't mean we don't feel the pain of emotional injustice or struggle with anger or bad memories. We do feel the pain. However, choosing the "more excellent way" means that we seek, by the power and with the help of the Holy Spirit within us, to honestly deal with our emotional wounds. We forgive others just as we have been forgiven many times over by Christ. We seek to understand the person who has caused us injury and acknowledge that we have done the same to others. We confess our own bad attitudes, self-pity, and unforgiving heart. We see things from God's perspective, and we refuse to carry on the fight. We pray, and we go to the other person seeking authentic restoration and healing.

Scripture provides many examples of the power of forgiving love. When David heard that King Saul, who had tried to kill him many times, had died in battle, he "mourned and wept and fasted until evening for Saul and for Jonathan his son" (2 Sam. 1:12). David didn't gloat over Saul's death, although most people in David's position would have danced for joy. At the cross Jesus prayed, "Father, forgive them, for they know not what they do" (Luke 23:34). And Stephen, the first Christian martyr, also prayed for forgiveness for his executioners: "Lord, do not hold this sin against them" (Acts 7:60).

Other believers continue to give us good examples of the power of forgiving love. After Jim Elliot and his four companions (Pete Fleming, Roger Youderian, Ed McCully, and Nate Saint) were killed by the Auca Indians in the Amazon jungle of eastern Ecuador, his wife Elisabeth and the four other wives thought not of revenge but of love and forgiveness. A reporter who witnessed their reaction to the news gave this account:

> The widows believed that their husbands' death was not the meaningless tragedy it appeared to many. No thoughts of revenge crossed their minds; on the contrary, they felt with an increased sense of urgency the need to bring their message of love and redemption to the Aucas.[6]

Elisabeth Elliot later wrote,

> It gives me a much more personal desire to reach them. The fact that Jesus Christ died for all makes me interested in the salvation of all, but the fact that Jim loved and died for the Aucas intensifies my love for them.[7]

Nearly three years after the deaths of the five young missionaries, Elisabeth Elliot and Rachel Saint moved into an Auca village, the first foreigners ever to live among this fierce people. These women became friends and gospel messengers to the very men who killed their husbands. Today, as a result of those first encounters and the work of later missionaries, the New Testament has been translated and a church established. It is a remarkable story of Christian love and forgiveness.

Clara Barton, founder of the American Red Cross and known as the "Angel of the Battlefield," was a remarkable woman of lionhearted courage and sterling character. Like any prominent person she had critics. When a friend of hers reminded Clara of the criticism someone had made of her work, Clara couldn't remember it. Surprised, her friend said, "You don't remember it?" Clara's response is classic: "No, I distinctly remember forgetting it." Love makes a point of forgetting wrongs suffered.

African-American evangelist and social reformer John Perkins relates how he and other friends had been beaten nearly to death and tortured in a Mississippi jail for trying to help black people gain social equality and economic independence. For hours on end he was brutally kicked and stomped on, hit with blackjacks and billy clubs until he was bleeding and unconscious. Inebriated police officers held an unloaded gun to his head and pulled the trigger to taunt him. One officer forced a fork down his throat. They gave full vent to their vile hatred. Two years later, John was convalescing from a stomach operation. He was still waiting for civil justice, but as he lay in bed, he reflected on the suffering he had experienced and what God would have him do. He wrote:

> I began to see with horror how hate could destroy me—destroy me more devastatingly and suddenly than any destruction I could bring on those who had wronged me. I could try and fight back, as many of my brothers had done. But if I did, how would I be different from the whites who hate?
>
> And where would hating get me? Anyone can hate. This whole business of hating and hating back … it's what keeps the vicious circle of racism going.
>
> The Spirit of God worked on me as I lay in that bed. An image formed in my mind. The image of the cross—Christ on the cross. It blotted out everything else in my mind.
>
> This Jesus knew what I had suffered. He understood. And He cared. Because He had experienced it all Himself.
>
> … And He prayed God to forgive them. "Father, forgive these people, for they don't know what they are doing."
>
> His enemies hated. But Jesus forgave. I couldn't get away from that.

The Spirit of God kept working on me and in me until I could say with Jesus, "I forgive them, too." I promised him that I would "return good for evil," not evil for evil. And he gave me the love I knew I would need to fulfill his command to me of "love your enemy."

Because of Christ, God himself met me and healed my heart and mind with his love.

… The Spirit of God helped me to really believe what I had so often professed, that only in the love of Christ is there any hope for me, or for those I had once worked so hard for.[8]

Life lived according to the "more excellent way" doesn't keep a journal of injustices and emotional hurts. It makes no plans to get even. Instead, "love is generous in her forgetfulness."[9] Love forgives and blesses those who have caused offense.

Love Does Not Rejoice in Wrongdoing

The eighth and final negative statement provides a perfect conclusion: Love "does not rejoice at wrongdoing" (1 Cor. 13:6). Love, writes Leon Morris, "takes no joy in evil of any kind."[10] Love cannot find distorted pleasure in injustice or unrighteousness because all such behavior hurts people and dishonors God. Love has no sympathetic attitude toward anything unrighteous. People who practice the "more excellent way" of love "abhor what is evil; hold fast to what is good" (Rom. 12:9).

In a secular world that often calls "evil good and good evil" (Isa. 5:20), there is, unfortunately, much joy over and approval of unrighteousness (Rom. 1:32). But it is astonishing how deeply "religious" people can also take great pleasure in wrongdoing. Those who masterminded the attacks on the World Trade Center in New York City on September 11, 2001, that killed and terrified thousands of innocent people relished their mission of death. Throughout the world, some people danced openly in delight while others gloated secretly. In the name of God and religion, people can lie, kill, and wage war.

Some Bible-believing Christians can also be found rejoicing in unrighteousness. An evangelical pastor, for example, announced gleefully from the pulpit that a brother in Christ who had opposed his ministry had died suddenly. He declared the man's death to be God's judgment. A deaconess spoke triumphantly to her friends of her success in driving out four different pastors through her phone calls and letter-writing campaigns. An elder bragged of enjoying a good fight and of humiliating his pastor and crushing the pastor's plans for the church. A pastor gloated when he heard of

> **"What a man rejoices in is a fair test of his character."**
> **—W. Graham Scroggie**

the misfortunes of people who had left his church. These "malignant joys" greatly grieve the Holy Spirit of God (Eph. 4:30). These are certainly not the behaviors of those who walk according to the "more excellent way" of love.

Scroggie is very perceptive when he says, "What a man rejoices in is a fair test of his character. To be glad when evil prevails, or to rejoice in the misfortunes of others is indicative of great moral degradation."[11]

Loving people do not take pleasure in feelings of superiority over others. They do not delight in juicy gossip nor do they find satisfaction in hearing about the sordid sins and demise of Christian leaders they don't like. They do not gloat over scandals in a denomination to which they once belonged nor do they take pleasure in the fact that people who left their church have met with misfortune. They cannot feel glad when an earthquake in a nation they despise results in thousands of deaths. They don't enjoy publicly denouncing or criticizing the failures and errors of other Christians. And if they must expose and confront sinful behavior, they do it with compassion and genuine sadness of heart.

Loving leaders walk in the example of Job and David. Job was a loving community elder who could honestly say to his detractors, "[I have not] rejoiced at the ruin of him who hated me, or exulted when evil overtook him" (Job 31:29). David found no joy in defeating his nemesis. He refused to rejoice over opportunities to kill Saul, his mortal enemy (1 Sam. 24:1-7). On more than one occasion when David could easily have killed the king, he spared his life. Even Saul was forced to admit to David, "You are more righteous than I, for you have repaid me good, whereas I have repaid you evil" (1 Sam. 24:17). Saul never did understand David's remarkable love for him and his family. Petty, jealous leaders do not give people the benefit of the doubt, and they are not in the habit of thinking the best about others.

Love Rejoices with the Truth

To the last negative statement, love "does not rejoice at wrongdoing," Paul adds a positive counterpart: Love "rejoices with the truth." A loving heart is saddened by wrongdoing because it destroys people and displeases God. But the truth has just the opposite effect—it makes love sing for joy like a morning bird on a summer day. Love quickly recognizes conduct and attitudes that accord with the truth and takes great pleasure when truth prevails.

In this context, the word *truth* is used in the sense of righteous behavior or principles of conduct that correspond to the truth of the gospel message. Paul speaks not of "truth" in the abstract, but truth in practice that results in righteous living. Truth and righteousness are welded together in Christian faith. Love applauds all virtue and goodness, whether the person is a believer or an unbeliever. It rejoices in holy character, righteous conduct, integrity, and growth in Christ. "The person full of Christian love joins in rejoicing on the side of behavior that reflects the gospel—for every victory gained, every forgiveness offered, every act of kindness."[12]

Leaders and teachers who love people will tell you that one of their greatest delights is seeing those they lead grow in the faith and live obedient lives for Christ. I remember once sitting with a group of Christian college professors and teachers in a cafeteria and listening to them talk. They rejoiced over the progress of their students' lives as if they were talking about their team winning a world soccer match. To watch their students live according to the truth was their joy.

The father of the prodigal son rejoiced with great joy over his son's righteous repentance and return home (Luke 15:11-32). Luke records,

> while he was still a long way off, his father saw him ... and ran and embraced him and kissed him.... The Father said to his servant, "Bring quickly the best robe, and put it on him, and put a ring on his hand, and shoes on his feet. And bring the fatted calf and kill it, and let us eat and celebrate." (Luke 15:20-23)

The prodigal's older brother, however, had no joy over his brother's repentance and homecoming because he did not have the love of God in his heart. Full of self-righteousness, "he was angry and refused to go in" to the celebration of his brother's homecoming. He would have rejoiced only at hearing of evil coming upon his brother or even of his death.

The tender heart of Paul rejoiced in all that the Corinthians did that was right and good, despite their many failures (1 Cor. 1:4-8; 11:2). He didn't inwardly gloat over God's discipline of some of the Corinthians for disobeying his instructions (1 Cor. 11:30). Their sufferings brought him no satisfaction or self-vindication. He could rejoice only at repentance, reconciliation, healing, godly conduct, and victory over the devil. To see his converts grow in love and walk in holy behavior delighted his heart.

John rejoiced over a brother named Gaius for living the Christian life according to the truth:

> For I rejoiced greatly when the brothers came and testified to your truth, as indeed you are walking in the truth. I have no greater joy than to hear that my children are walking in the truth. Beloved, it is a faithful thing you do in all your efforts for these brothers, strangers as they are, who testified to your love before the church. (3 John 3-6; also 2 John 4)

The proof that Gaius walked in the truth was the loving hospitality he showed to traveling Christians, most of whom were itinerate evangelists and teachers (3 John 5-8). It gave John great joy to hear that Gaius was kind, generous, and selfless.

Rejoicing in the truth, not wrongdoing, is living according to the "more excellent way" of love.

Notes to Chapter 8

1. Robert L. Peterson and Alexander Strauch, *Agape Leadership: Lessons in Spiritual Leadership from the Life of R. C. Chapman* (Littleton, Colo.: Lewis & Roth, 1991), 39.

2. David E. Garland, *1 Corinthians,* BECNT (Grand Rapids, Mich.: Baker, 2003), 618-19.

3. D. A. Carson, *Showing the Spirit: A Theological Exposition of 1 Corinthians* 12–14 (Grand Rapids, Mich.: Baker, 1987), 62.

4. Jay E. Adams, *Christian Living in the Home* (Grand Rapids, Mich.: Baker, 1972), 33.

5. Lewis Smedes, *Love within Limits: Realizing Selfless Love in a Selfish World* (Grand Rapids, Mich.: Eerdmans, 1978), 78-79.

6. Elisabeth Elliot, *The Savage My Kinsman* (Ann Arbor, Mich.: Servant Books, 1981), 6.

7. Ibid., 9.

8. John Perkins, *Let Justice Roll Down* (Glendale, Calif.: Regal Books, 1976), 204-06.

9. W. Graham Scroggie, *The Love Life: A Study of 1 Corinthians 13* (London: Pickering & Inglis, n.d.), 44.

10. Leon Morris, *The First Epistle of Paul to the Corinthians,* TNTC (Grand Rapids, Mich.: Eerdmans, 1958), 185.

11. Scroggie, *The Love Life,* 45.

12. Gordon D. Fee, *The First Epistle to the Corinthians,* NICNT (Grand Rapids, Mich.: Eerdmans, 1987), 639.

Chapter 9

Bears, Believes, Hopes, and Endures All Things

Love bears all things, believes all things, hopes all things, endures all things.

1 Cor. 13:7

Love is tenacious. I once read a story of a criminally minded young man who continually got in trouble with the police for drugs and stealing. He was arrested and jailed several times and eventually was sent to prison for much of his remaining life. After a short time in prison, he was forgotten by his friends and even by his father. Outside the walls of his prison cell, he was a forgotten human being except for one person. Every week his mother would board a bus and travel several hours to visit him in prison. After a few hours of visitation, she would board the bus and return home. Almost daily she wrote letters and often sent books and personal items as allowed by prison officials. Neither distance, prison walls, money, or time could stop her from loving and visiting her son.

Some people think that loving people are weak and spineless. But nothing could be further from the truth. Unloving people are the ones who are weak because they are controlled by their petty, self-centered cravings. Jesus was the most loving person who ever existed, and he was not weak. He gave his life to save others. Paul's continual pursuit of the Corinthians after all the heartache they had caused him demonstrated not weakness but rather great strength and endurance.

81

The Tenacious Power of Love

Paul concludes and summarizes his description of love with four short, positive clauses that tell us what love does.[1] Love bears all things, believes all things, hopes all things, endures all things.

Bears All Things

Love bears up[2] under the heavy load of life's problems and sufferings. It holds steadfast and remains strong despite opposition, deprivation, and hard work.

Loving leaders persevere and do not give up easily or fall apart under pressure.

Love is courageous. It can carry enormous weight; thus loving leaders have an amazing ability to endure all sorts of suffering and frustration for the sake of others and the gospel (1 Cor. 9:12). This is a trait of all good shepherds (Gen. 31:38-40). They persevere and do not give up easily or fall apart under pressure.

Believes All Things

Paul next brings out faith and hope because of their connection with bearing and enduring all things. Faith and hope are the components of love that enable it to endure hardship and to bear up under the heavy burdens of life. In dealing with loved ones, love is not suspicious or cynical, but open and favorably disposed toward them. It seeks to understand each person in the best light with an understanding of life's complexities. It believes people can change and improve. It sees their worth, potential, and future possibilities. "It studies motives, and makes all possible allowances,"[3] says Scroggie. It is not afraid of being proved wrong or being embarrassed by others.

This doesn't imply that love is credulous or blind, for that would be a spurious faith. It is understood, although not directly stated, that love does not believe lies. Jesus' dealings with the Twelve, with their weaknesses and their failures, demonstrate the Christlike love that believes and hopes all things.

Love also trusts God and his Word and this makes all the difference in how one views and responds to people and difficult problems. Faith views people and life through the lens of God's sovereign purposes for his people.

Faith rests assured that "all things work together for good" for those who love God (Rom. 8:28). It believes nothing can "separate us from the love of God in Christ Jesus our Lord" (Rom. 8:39); "he who began a good work in you will bring it to completion at the day of Jesus Christ" (Phil. 1:6), and nothing is impossible with God.

Hopes All Things

The other core ingredient of love is hope. The situation in the church at Corinth was a mess, but Paul never gives up hope. He doesn't despair. He doesn't walk away from them in frustration. He writes letters, he visits, he sends representatives, and he prays. Despite his stern words, he has confidence that they eventually would respond properly.

Paul expresses his confidence in them: "I have great pride in you; I am filled with comfort. In all our affliction, I am overflowing with joy" (2 Cor. 7:4). "I rejoice, because I have perfect confidence in you" (2 Cor. 7:16; see also 1:7; 2:3; 7:4; 14-16; 10:15).

This confidence is not a sentimental wish; it is faith in God's ultimate triumph and in God's good intentions for his people. This gives him realistic optimism and confidence in the future, even in the face of repeated difficulties and disappointments. Hope in the Lord and trust in his sure promises enable Paul to put problems and failures in perspective (Gal. 5:10; 2 Thess. 3:4; Philem. 21).

> **Faith in God's ultimate triumph and in God's good intentions for his people gives realistic optimism even in the face of repeated difficulties and disappointments.**

Endures All Things

This last quality, endurance, is similar to the first, "bears all things." Love is strong and tenacious: "No hardship or rebuff ever makes love cease to be love."[4] Love lasts; it holds out; it perseveres in the face of opposition, unkindness, and difficulties; it never gives up. Serving Christ and his people cannot be done without labor and self-sacrifice. Love gives a person the power to endure all things.

The life of Moses, Israel's greatest leader, illustrates that love bears up, believes, hopes, and endures all things. For forty trying years, he led the nation of Israel through the desert of Sinai. The people repeatedly complained about his leadership. They falsely accused him of abuse, ineptitude, evil motives, pride, and even trying to kill them and their children. At one time they were ready to stone him to death. Here are a few examples of their accusations and complaints:

- "Is it because there are no graves in Egypt that you have taken us away to die in the wilderness? What have you done to us in bringing us out of Egypt? ... Leave us alone that we may serve the Egyptians." (Ex. 14:11-12)
- And the whole congregation of the people of Israel grumbled against Moses and Aaron.... "You have brought us out into this wilderness to kill this whole assembly with hunger." (Ex. 16:2-3)
- The people quarreled with Moses.... So Moses cried to the Lord, "What shall I do with this people? They are almost ready to stone me." (Ex. 17:2-4)
- "Our wives and our little ones will become a prey. Would it not be better for us to go back to Egypt?" And they said to one another, "Let us choose a leader and go back to Egypt." (Num. 14:3-4)
- "Why have you made us come up out of Egypt to bring us to this evil place?" (Num. 20:5)

On one occasion his brother and sister spoke evil against him (Num. 12). They said, "Has the Lord indeed spoken only through Moses? Has he not spoken through us also" (Num. 12:2). It must have been particularly painful for Moses when his own family and closest confidants attacked him. Yet he forgave them and prayed for their restoration after God judged them for their sinful accusations.

One of the worst moments of Moses' life was when 250 prominent leaders of the nation accused him of sinful, dominating leadership (Num. 16). They said to Moses and Aaron,

You have gone too far! ... Why then do you exalt yourselves above the assembly of the Lord? ... Is it a small thing that you have brought us up out of a land ... to kill us in the wilderness, that you must also make yourself a prince over us? Moreover, you have not brought us into a land flowing with milk and honey. (Num. 16:3, 13-14)

The people outright rejected Moses' authority and appointed a new leader to guide them back to Egypt (Neh. 9:17). On this occasion, Moses prayed to God to punish them for their wickedness, and God did. Their punishment was just and long overdue.

At other times, however, Moses prayed that God would not destroy the people. On four different occasions God was about to destroy the whole nation because of their continual rebellion, but Moses prayed and pleaded with God to spare them.[5] Moses probably could have thought of a hundred reasons not to pray for them, but as a man of God he was able to rise above personal feelings and pray for their forgiveness and deliverance.

Only love for God and love for the people could explain Moses' forbearance with the children of Israel. Love suffers long, love endures all things, love believes all things, and love hopes all things. Time after time, when it appeared that all was lost for the nation, Moses trusted, hoped, and endured. Selfish leaders, on the other hand, melt like snowflakes when the heat is on. They do not persevere.

Most significant ministry with people is usually long-term, but long-term ministry succeeds only with supernatural power from above to endure all of life's hardships and heartaches. Some missionaries serve for decades in dangerous areas where the problems and setbacks never end. How do they last? The answer: love for God and love for people. Love generates the faith, hope, and endurance to persevere through a lifetime of problems.

The Greatest Thing in the World

Love's power to endure (1 Cor. 13:7) leads to the final section of chapter 13 (vv. 9-13), where Paul makes two of his most profound declarations about Christian love: "Love never ends" and "faith, hope, and love abide, these three; but the greatest of these is love."

Love Is Eternal
1 Cor. 13:8-12

In verse 8, Paul writes, "Love never ends." Technically this is not part of the fifteen descriptions of love in verses 4 through 7. Verse 8 begins a new section that contrasts the temporary nature of spiritual gifts with the permanent nature of love. This brings Paul directly back to his concern over the misuse of spiritual gifts in the church at Corinth (1 Cor. 12:1–13:3).

To show again that love is the "more excellent way," Paul tells his readers that spiritual gifts, no matter how impressive and important they appear, will someday cease: "As for prophecies, they will pass away; as for tongues, they will cease; as for knowledge, it will pass away" (1 Cor. 13:8). There will come a day when spiritual gifts will no longer be needed and will cease. We will not need spiritual gifts in heaven.

Heaven will be a home filled forever with love because God is there and "God is love."

They are for the present age only. Love, in contrast, will never come to an end. It is for now and eternity.

In the concluding chapter of *Charity and Its Fruits*, Jonathan Edwards describes heaven as "a world of holy love"[6] and "the paradise of love."[7] Heaven will be a home filled forever with love because God is there and "God is love" (1 John 4:8).

When Christians love one another as Jesus did, the local church family prefigures the glories of our future loving, heavenly existence. Sadly, the church at Corinth was not experiencing heavenly love. It was characterized by rivalries, lawsuits, immorality, abuse of Christian liberty, disorderly conduct, pride, and selfish independence—altogether an unacceptably poor representation of the heavenly realities of love and the fruit of the Spirit.

Love Is the Greatest Virtue
1 Cor. 13:13

The chapter closes with the familiar words: "So now faith, hope, and love abide, these three; but the greatest of these is love" (1 Cor. 13:13). Not every Christian is gifted with prophecy, tongues, or knowledge, but every Christian must be characterized by faith, hope, and love. This triad of virtues is fundamental to living the Christian life and to the maturing of the local church (1 Thess. 1:2-3).

Yet even among the three cardinal virtues of faith, hope, and love, Paul can say, "the greatest of these is love." So whether we are talking about spiritual gifts or cardinal virtues, love is the greatest! This is why every Christian leader and teacher must actively and intentionally "pursue love" (1 Cor. 14:1).

Summary of the Character and Behavior
of a Loving Leader

Applying Paul's fifteen descriptions of love, we who lead and teach God's people are to be marked first by patience and kindness, even when we are wronged by those we serve. Our entire ministry is to be characterized by patience and kindness.

We are not to be self-centered leaders who are envious of those who are more talented or more popular than we are. Nor are we to put others down or boast about our own achievements. Most important, we are never to be arrogant and think of ourselves as superior to other people. We are to be humble and modest. We are not to be rude or ill-mannered but always tactful and conscious of proper social decorum. We are especially not to be self-seekers who look out first and foremost for our own interests and advantage. We are to be servants who build others up. We are not to be easily provoked to anger or irritability, which can be emotionally damaging to those we lead. We are to be calm, slow to anger, and never vindictive. We must not hold grudges but rather forgive and be gracious. Finally, we are not to rejoice in wrongdoing of any kind, but we are to rejoice with the truth.

We must always remember that love bears all things, believes all things, hopes all things, and endures all things.

A Plea for Self-Examination

I close this section with an important personal plea: Do not use this book to tell other people they have no love. Some of the most loving people I have ever known have been wrongfully accused of a lack of love.

In the Old Testament, the children of Israel accused Moses of unloving domination of the people, although he had saved their lives on many occasions and poured himself out to lead them for forty years. The truth is, the children of Israel were the unloving ones.

Most often, people who say that others have no love are themselves the ones most lacking. They think the new commandment says, "Love me or I'll destroy you and your church." They sit around waiting for other people to love them.

How easy it is to see the speck of lovelessness in another's eye but miss the log of self-centeredness, hypocrisy, and anger in your own eye (Matt. 7: 3-5). *Use this book, therefore, to speak to yourself.* Strive to be an example to others of love according to the "more excellent way." And when a situation arises that demands confronting loveless behavior, you will have credibility as well as the skill to confront, "speaking the truth in love" (Eph. 4:15).

If we are honest, we must admit that we all have failed to love as we ought. So we should judge ourselves first. Only after we have confessed and repented of our own sins of lovelessness can we begin to help others to love. A good way to do that is to pray for them, because only God can change hearts.

Of course, even loving people do unloving things at times. They get into terrible conflicts and are not what they should be. Martin Luther, the sixteenth-century reformer, was a selfless, loving man, but he could also at times be cutting and harsh. The only perfectly loving person to grace this earth was the Lord Jesus Christ. The rest of us struggle all our lives to love as he loved and to figure out exactly how to love in difficult situations.

Notes to Chapter 9

1. Each of the four verbs has as its object the Greek word *panta*, "all things." However, the accusative case here "stands almost in the sense of an adverb": "always" or "in everything" (BDAG, s.v. *pas*, 783). The NIV and a number of commentators prefer this adverbial rendering. This avoids the idea that love gullibly believes "all things" and hopes "all things." It is difficult to be certain of the translation.

2. The Greek verb *stegō* can mean either (1) "covers," as in covering another's faults (NIV: "protects") or (2) "bears up under difficulty." Either meaning is possible here; however, the latter follows Paul's usage (1 Cor. 9:12; 1 Thess. 3:1, 5) and is favored.

3. W. Graham Scroggie, *The Love Life: A Study of 1 Corinthians 13* (London: Pickering & Inglis, n.d.), 46.

4. C. K. Barrett, *A Commentary on the First Epistle to the Corinthians*, HNTC (New York: Harper & Row, 1968), 305.

5. Ex. 32:10-14; Num. 14:12-20; 16:20-22, 41-50.

6. Jonathan Edwards, *Charity and Its Fruits* (1852; reprint ed., Edinburgh: Banner of Truth, 1978), 325.

7. Ibid., 351.

Part Three

The Works of a Loving Leader

Chapter 10

Expressing Love and Affection

*I hold you in my heart.... I yearn for you all
with the affection of Christ Jesus.*
Phil. 1:7-8

A family friend attended a Bible-teaching church but moved away for several years. When she returned, she noticed a wonderful, exciting change. The church was still a Bible-teaching church, but over the years it had grown in love. The people were friendlier, more welcoming, and hospitable. They hugged one another, they were more caring, and they took care of needy members. An atmosphere of loving affection was palpable throughout the congregation.

Putting Love in Words

The love in this church was seen in words, deeds, and displays of affection. The fact is, *love must express itself; it cannot remain silent.* When his Son was on the earth, the Father cried out from heaven, "This is my beloved Son, with whom I am well pleased" (Matt. 3:17). Jesus verbally expressed his love for his Father and his disciples: "I love the Father" (John 14:31); "so have I loved you" (John 15:9). Jesus asked Peter, "Do you love me?" Three times Peter replied, "I love you" (John 21:15-17).

Expressions of heartfelt love such as these set the tone for the entire New Testament.

Expressing Gratitude

Loving people are full of gratitude and they express it openly. Of all the New Testament writers, Paul most frequently speaks of his love for his co-workers and converts. Throughout his letters, Paul freely expresses appreciation and recognizes his fellow workers for their service to him and to God for the sake of the gospel. He does not hold back acknowledgment and praise. He is deeply grateful for all of them and everything they have done.

Romans 16 provides an extended example of Paul's lavish public praise for personal friendships and the works of others:

- Phoebe, a servant of the church (Rom. 16:1)
- Prisca and Aquila … who risked their necks for my life (Rom. 16:3-4)
- Mary, who has worked hard for you (Rom. 16:6)
- Andronicus and Junia … well known to the apostles (Rom. 16:7)
- Ampliatus, my beloved in the Lord (Rom. 16:8)
- Apelles, who is approved in Christ (Rom. 16:10)
- Tryphaena and Tryphosa, workers in the Lord (Rom. 16:12)
- The beloved Persis, who has worked hard in the Lord (Rom. 16:12)
- Rufus, chosen in the Lord (Rom. 16:13)
- Gaius … host to me and to the whole church (Rom. 16:23)

Other letters of Paul provide further examples:

- The household of Stephanas … [who] devoted themselves to the service of the saints (1 Cor. 16:15)
- Tychicus … faithful minister in the Lord (Eph. 6:21)
- But you know of Timothy's proven worth (Phil. 2:22)
- Epaphroditus my brother and fellow worker and fellow soldier (Phil. 2:25)
- Epaphras our beloved fellow servant … a faithful minister of Christ on your behalf (Col. 1:7)
- Tychicus … a faithful minister and fellow servant in the Lord (Col. 4:7)

- Onesimus, our faithful and beloved brother (Col. 4:9)
- Epaphras ... a servant of Christ Jesus ... always struggling on your behalf in his prayers (Col. 4:12)
- Luke the beloved physician (Col. 4:14)
- Titus, my true child in a common faith (Titus 1:4)
- Philemon our beloved fellow worker ... the hearts of the saints have been refreshed through you (Philem. 1, 7)

God is verbal, and he created us to be verbal creatures. So in our ministry we must learn to be generous with our words of praise and thanks. We need to let people know we are thankful to God for them. They should not be left guessing about what we think. They need to hear from us.

Leaders who speak only when there is something negative to say or to disapprove are not effective. People need to hear positive words of appreciation and love—such words build healthy Christian community. Just as people need oxygen in order to breathe, they need a fresh breath of affirmation and acknowledgement to nurture their souls. As leaders, we should aspire to be like Barnabas, who continually encouraged other people with Scripture and with gracious words of affirmation.

I know of a couple who spent thirty-five years voluntarily serving as Sunday school superintendents in a local church. Many in leadership admitted this couple was irreplaceable, but when they retired, no one even said thank you. There was no public acknowledgment; there were no phone calls or letters of appreciation. They were devastated by silent ingratitude, and understandably so! Members of the body of Christ should relate to one another in active community, not passive isolation.

> **Leaders who speak only when there is something negative to say or to disapprove are not effective. People need to hear positive words of appreciation and love.**

The church should be a place where people express love and appreciation, thank one another, and encourage one another.

Expressing Heartfelt Love

To his converts, Paul often expresses deep affection through intensely emotional words. He writes with the voice of a tender shepherd, not that of an aloof professional religious official or hardened zealot interested only in the cause. Even when he corrects and disciplines Paul is fatherly and pastoral, tender and tearful, sympathetic and caring. Notice how many verses there are that express his loving heart and affectionate leadership style:

- I rejoice over you. (Rom. 16:19)
- I hold you in my heart. (Phil. 1:7)
- I yearn for you all with the affection of Christ Jesus. (Phil. 1:8)
- My brothers, whom I love and long for, my joy and crown. (Phil. 4:1)
- Being affectionately desirous of you, we were ready to share with you not only the gospel of God but also our own selves, because you had become very dear to us. (1 Thess. 2:8)
- My little children, for whom I am again in the anguish of childbirth until Christ is formed in you, I wish I could be present with you now. (Gal. 4:19-20)
- My love be with you all in Christ Jesus. (1 Cor. 16:24)
- I wrote to you out of much affliction and anguish of heart and with many tears ... to let you know the abundant love that I have for you. (2 Cor. 2:4)
- We have spoken freely to you, Corinthians; our heart is wide open. (2 Cor. 6:11)
- You are in our hearts, to die together and to live together. (2 Cor. 7:3)
- Because I do not love you? God knows I do! (2 Cor. 11:11)
- I seek not what is yours but you. (2 Cor. 12:14)
- I will most gladly spend and be spent for your souls. If I love you more, am I to be loved less? (2 Cor. 12:15)
- And may the Lord make you increase ... in love for one another ... as we do for you. (1 Thess. 3:12)
- I am sending him back to you, sending my very heart. (Philem. 12)

Paul expressed his deep-seated affection for his converts by his generous use of terms of endearment. No less than twenty-four times Paul addresses his readers as "beloved."[1] It is no empty platitude or mere politeness. The term expresses intimacy, affection, and love. Paul's friends and converts were his dearly beloved brothers and sisters. They were his family. They were bound intimately together by the same Spirit. Beloved of God,[2] they were also beloved of Paul.

Leaders and teachers in the church should not be reluctant to use loving family language to express the reality of their relationship to one another. This was the normal practice of the early Christians. The terms *brothers, brother,* or *sister* occur approximately 250 times throughout the New Testament. In an ancient Christian dialogue, a Latin work titled Octavius, the pagan Caecilius criticized the Christians because "hardly have they met when they love each other.... Indiscriminately they call each other brother and sister."[3] What a blessing it would be for us to be so accused! People today as much as ever need to hear words of family love and connectedness. Such intimate, familial language is biblical, and it reflects the love of the New Testament church.

Showing Physical Signs of Affection

One physical expression of Christian love is the "kiss of love," and it is "one of the beautiful customs of the early Christians."[4] Peter urged his readers to "Greet one another with the kiss of love" (1 Peter 5:14), which is a practical outworking of his earlier instructions to love one another fervently as brothers and sisters:

- Love one another earnestly from a pure heart (1 Peter 1:22)
- Love the brotherhood (1 Peter 2:17)
- Above all, keep loving one another earnestly (1 Peter 4:8)

This "kiss of love," which Paul also refers to as a "holy kiss,"[5] is an outward, physical sign of "mutuality ... oneness of status and identity which all Christians share across divisions of race, class, and gender."[6] But it is a "holy" kiss, not a sensual kiss. It is to be expressed with respect and in all purity.

Whether we apply the "kiss of love" with an actual kiss, hug, or hearty handshake, we are commanded to greet brothers and sisters affectionately. Our greetings to one another should visibly express the reality of our family oneness and love. So let us not be impersonal, standoffish, or cold. Let us not take one another for granted. People need physical expressions of love as well as words of love. This physical expression of love is one concrete, practical way we live out the New Testament command to love "one another earnestly" (1 Peter 4:8).

John Stott, a naturally reserved and proper Englishman, has learned from his extensive world travels, especially to Latin America and Africa, to enjoy the affectionate physical embrace of fellow believers. In closing a letter to a friend, he quips: I "send you a greeting and a hug (I'm now a life-member of the Institute of Hug Therapy!)."[7]

Paul too was a member of the "Institute of Hug Therapy." At the end of Paul's farewell message to the Ephesian elders, Luke records: "And there was much weeping on the part of all; they embraced Paul and kissed him" (Acts 20:37).

The children in our churches need to feel expressions of love too. Our Lord Jesus welcomed children. They were a joy to him. He was not too busy to pay attention to them. He touched, prayed for, and blessed them (Matt. 19:13-15). Mothers and children felt comfortable coming to Jesus because his nature was welcoming and affectionate. Let us also be protective of and loving toward children.

The local church is "the household of God" (1 Tim. 3:15) and should be filled with loving words and demonstrations of familial affection. Sadly, the atmosphere in some churches is more like a funeral home than a loving family home. There is little affection and warmth.

Don't take anyone for granted. God doesn't!

Legitimate emotional feelings are suffocated. People hardly know one another. They keep their distance, and the only display of affection is a speedy handshake before exiting the church doors. Such behavior is not authentic Christian brotherhood and sisterhood. It does not represent people who are faithful to the "new commandment."

How to Get Started

To create a more loving atmosphere in your local church or in a group you lead, start by regularly praying for growth in love. Use these Scriptures as a guide in your prayers:

- And it is my prayer that your love may abound more and more. (Phil. 1:9)
- And may the Lord make you increase and abound in love for one another and for all. (1 Thess. 3:12)
- [I pray] that you ... may have strength to comprehend with all the saints what is the breadth and length and height and depth, and to know the love of Christ that surpasses knowledge. (Eph. 3:18-19)

Even if your church or group is a loving body, you always can excel still "more and more" in love (1 Thess. 4:10). Teach what the Bible says about love. How often do people hear a careful exposition of 1 Corinthians 13, Ephesians 3:14-19 and 4:1-16, or 1 John 4:7-21? Most church-goers do not know the biblical demands of love and need in-depth teaching on this subject. Challenge the people you lead to grow in love.

An atmosphere of love doesn't come by teaching alone. Church leaders need to model love. There are teachers, musicians, and others in the church who have voluntarily served for years. They need to know that their faithfulness to God and the congregation is appreciated. Express your gratitude to them and encourage others to do the same. There are people who clean, repair, and maintain the church building; don't let them go unnoticed. They should be thanked verbally or with a gift or card. Don't take anyone for granted. God doesn't!

> **The church is to be a life-transforming community where people grow and become more like their loving Lord.**

Don't allow your church to be a place where members of the body of Christ have only superficial interaction, or worse, where they come and go without even speaking to one another. Again, it is your responsibility to lead by example. The church is not a business corporation, military institution, or government agency. It is the "household of God," so act accordingly. Reach out to others in love. Greet them with a "kiss of love," an affectionate hug, or a "holy handshake." Make it a point to remember people's names.

The church is to be a close-knit family of brothers and sisters who express Christ's love to one another. It is to be a life-transforming community where people grow and become more like their loving Lord. Your church can become a more loving community and experience greater unity as you teach and lead with love.

Notes to Chapter 10

1. The term *beloved* is used nine times by John, seven by Peter, three by James, and three by Jude.

2. Rom. 1:7; 1 Thess. 1:4; 2 Thess. 2:13.

3. *The Octavius of Marcus Minucius Felix*, in *Ancient Christian Writers*, eds. Johannes Quasten et al., trans. G. W. Clarke (New York: Newman, 1974), 64.

4. Paul A. Cedar, *James; 1, 2 Peter; and Jude,* The Communicator's Commentary (Waco, Tex.: Word, 1984), 11:200.

5. Rom. 16:16; 1 Cor. 16:20; 2 Cor. 13:12; 1 Thess. 5:26.

6. Anthony C. Thiselton, *The First Epistle to the Corinthians*, NIGTC (Grand Rapids, Mich.: Eerdmans, 2000), 1346.

7. Timothy Dudley-Smith, *John Stott: A Global Ministry* (Leicester, England: InterVarsity, 2001), 441.

Chapter 11

Practicing Hospitality

Let brotherly love continue. Do not neglect to show hospitality....
Heb. 13:1-2

Hardly anything is more characteristic of Christian love than hospitality. Hospitality is essential to fanning the flames of love and strengthening the Christian community. The Christian leader who offers hospitality to others fleshes out love in a uniquely personal way.

Through the ministry of hospitality, we share the things we value most: family, home, financial resources, food, privacy, and time. In other words, we share our lives.

Since Scripture repeatedly commands Christians to love one another, it should come as no surprise that Scripture also commands us to practice hospitality:

- Let love be genuine.... Love one another with brotherly affection ... and seek to show hospitality. (Rom. 12:9-10, 13)
- Above all, keep loving one another earnestly.... Show hospitality to one another without grumbling. (1 Peter 4:8-9)
- Let brotherly love continue. Do not neglect to show hospitality to strangers, for thereby some have entertained angels unawares. (Heb. 13:1-2)
- Beloved, it is a faithful thing you do in all your efforts for these brothers, strangers as they are, who testified to your [hospitality] before the church. (3 John 5-6)

Hospitality Creates Loving Community

A cold, unwelcoming church contradicts the gospel message. Yet unfriend-liness stands out as a frequent criticism of local churches.[1] It doesn't take people long to figure out there is a "churchy" love among Christians that ends at the back door of the sanctuary or in the parking lot. It is a superfi-cial, Sunday-morning-only kind of love that is unwilling to extend itself beyond the walls of the church building.

But Scripture tells us, "Love one another with brotherly affection" (Rom. 12:10). Brotherly love entails knowing one another and sharing life together. Unless we open the doors of our homes to one another, the reality of the local church as a close-knit family of loving brothers and sisters is just one more empty religious theory. It is impossible to know or grow close to our brothers and sisters by meet-ing for an hour a week with a large

Through the ministry of hospitality we provide the fellowship and care that nurtures true brotherly and sisterly love.

group in a church sanctuary. It is through the ministry of hospitality that we provide the fellowship and care that nurtures true brotherly and sisterly love.

In most instances, we hardly even know one another until we spend time together in one another's homes and talk across the table. A plaque on the wall of a restaurant beautifully expresses this point: "It is around a table that friends perceive best the warmth of being together." Therefore, when we speak of loving one another with brotherly affection we must also speak of practicing hospitality (Rom. 12:10, 13).

As an example of the effect hospitality has in communicating love and the familial nature of the local church, consider the story about a news re-porter who visited Christian churches to see how friendly and loving they were. He rated his visitation experiences according to this point system: The greeters at the door got two points. The prepackaged form letter from the pastor got three points. The coffee hour got five points. People intro-ducing themselves in a cordial, non-threatening way got ten points. But personal invitations to dinner got sixty points![2] The reporter's rating system shows how powerfully hospitality communicates love.

The nature of love is to welcome loved ones, to seek to be near them, and to share one's best with them. Love does not isolate itself, it extends itself. As leaders, we are to practice hospitality. Our homes are one of the best tools we have for building loving Christian community. By regularly opening our homes to others, we can help our local church (or group) become a more friendly, caring community.

Hospitality Aids Teaching and Discipleship

Shepherding people cannot be done from a distance, with a smile and a handshake on Sunday morning. It requires close interaction. The home can provide a powerfully effective setting in which to teach, disciple, and care for people.

Teaching the Scriptures in a comfortable home environment is highly conducive to learning God's Word (Acts 5:42; 20:20). Martin Luther proved that the table is a splendid pulpit from which to teach God's truths and disciple God's people. Luther and his wife, Katie, were widely known for their open home and liberal hospitality. One historian writes, "For the great house was always full to the brim."[3] Luther's famous *Table Talk,* written by their many students and guests, is a wonderful testimony to the power of the home in discipling and teaching people.

Although the ministry of hospitality may seem like a small thing, it has a great impact on people. An open home is a sign of an open, caring heart and a generous, giving spirit. Showing love to people, many of whom are hurting, by inviting them to your home for a meal or for counsel is deeply touching. Caring for God's people means, among other things, sharing your home with them for meals, encouraging friendly visits, or even providing temporary living accomodations.

> In his own mysterious way, God uses the mutual relationship between host and guest to instruct and encourage his people.

We must not underestimate the power of hospitality in teaching and caring for people. In his own mysterious way, God uses the mutual relationship between host and guest to instruct and encourage his people. This is one reason the New Testament requires a church elder to be "hospitable" (1 Tim. 3:1-2; Titus 1:7).

One of the great evangelists and church planters of the twentith century was Brother Bakht Singh of India. Shortly after his conversion to Christ from atheism and Hinduism, the Lord used the generous hospitality of John and Edith Haywards to disciple Bakht Singh. He lived with the Haywards in Winnipeg, Canada, for nearly three years. Little did they know of the impact their Indian friend would have on a nation. Bakht Singh's biographer, T. E. Koshy, credits "the important role of Christian homes in discipling and preparing new Christians as effective witnesses for the Lord."[4] He writes:

> The Lord used the Haywards greatly to mature him spiritually. While in their home, the Lord taught him various important lessons, including his total commitment to the Lord; accepting the Bible as the inspired Word of God; the importance of hospitality and prayer, as well as finding God's will for everything. Moreover, the Lord ministered to his temporal needs through this loving and caring Christian couple. The Haywards had opened their home to missionaries on furlough. This gave Bakht Singh opportunity to meet and to have fellowship with many godly people from various denominations and backgrounds.[5]

Hospitality Promotes Evangelism

Hospitality reaches out not only to believers but also to unbelievers. The nature of love is to reach out, to save, and to share the message of salvation. Loving leaders have a burden for the lost (Rom. 9:1-3; 10:1), and love for lost people compels us to practice hospitality. Hospitality is an effective means of reaching the lost.

For the early Christians, the home was the most natural setting for proclaiming Christ to families, neighbors, and friends. Michael Green, author of *Evangelism in the Early Church,* describes the home as "one of the most important methods of spreading the gospel in antiquity."[6] Referring to the home of Aquila and Priscilla, he writes, "Homes like this must have been exceedingly effective in the evangelistic outreach of the church."[7]

The same is true today. If you are looking for ways to evangelize, opening your home is one of the best methods of reaching unbelievers. Many of us don't even know our neighbors, yet through hospitality, we can make the most of every opportunity the Lord gives us to be his ambassadors to the world. If we are willing, our homes can be lighthouses in otherwise spiritually dark neighborhoods.

The founder of The Navigators, Dawson Trotman, for example, used his home to win military people to Christ. After several years of generous hospitality to sailors, he could say that sailors from every state in the United States of America had become Christians in his living room.

Jim Petersen, in his book *Evangelism as a Lifestyle,* tells about a Brazilian man, Mario, with whom he studied the Bible for four years before the young man came to Christ. Mario was a Marxist intellectual and political activist—an unlikely candidate for Christianity. Several years after Mario's conversion, Mario asked Jim if he knew what had made him decide for Christ. Jim thought it might be their many hours of intellectual discussion of Scripture, but here is Mario's reply:

> Remember that first time I stopped by your house? We were on our way someplace together and I had a bowl of soup with you and your family. As I sat there observing you, your wife, your children, and how you related to each other, I asked myself, *When will I have a relationship like this with my fiancée?* When I realized the answer was "never," I concluded I had to become a Christian for the sake of my own survival.[8]

Showing love to unbelievers by inviting them into your home is a powerful magnet for bringing people to Christ. You don't have to be a preacher or have years of training to use your home to love and serve people. If you simply open the doors of your home, the people will come.

How to Get Started

Our fast-paced, urbanized world leaves little time for hospitality. So here are a few ideas to help you obey the command of Scripture to practice hospitality (Rom. 12:13).

First, set a regular time each week or month to invite people to your home. Unless you plan this into your schedule, you may never move past good intentions to taking action. You'll think, *This is important. The Bible tells us to do this, and it will help our church.* But unless you plan ahead and make hospitality a priority, you'll find yourself busy next week, and the next week, and the week after that.

Second, make a list of people who would be encouraged by your offer of hospitality. For example, it could be a crucial step in helping new church members feel that they are welcomed as a part of the body. Those who are going through heavy trials may be encouraged simply by receiving an invitation. Many people

"Christian hospitality is not a matter of choice; it is not a matter of money ... age, social standing, sex, or personality. Christian hospitality is a matter of obedience to God."

—Helga Henry

are lonely and in need of love. In effect, you can be a ministering angel to those who are hurting.

Third, remember to invite people to your home during holiday seasons. These are especially good times to invite lonely people and nonChristian friends. Seek to include someone who rarely receives an invitation because of an infirmity. Be mindful of Jesus' teaching, "when you give a feast, invite the poor, the crippled, the lame, the blind, and you will be blessed, because they cannot repay you" (Luke 14:13).

Fourth, enjoy creative activities with your guests. Go around the dinner table asking some key questions of each person so that everyone gets to know one another. Have a time of prayer together, read Scripture together, or sing together. After the meal, take a walk together. All of these activities will draw you and your guests closer to each other and ultimately to the Lord.

Fifth, teach on the subject of hospitality. When did you last hear a message from Scripture on hospitality? People need to be taught the duty and the blessings of using their home for Christ. It's easy to forget to practice hospitality, so we all need to be reminded and exhorted.

Sixth, volunteer to house missionaries or traveling servants of the Lord. Some mission organizations have a list of host homes that missionaries use during their travels. You could find a compatible organization and sign up to be a host home. And when your church's missionaries return home, don't miss the opportunity to invite them to your table for a meal.

Your children especially will profit when you invite God's servants into your home. The late radio preacher and author Stephen Olford, born of missionary parents in Africa, gives his childhood impressions of his parents' generous hospitality:

No one can ever predict what eternal reward will be awaiting us for Christian hospitality. But even now there is a compensation in store for us. Hospitality is a thrilling adventure and brings wonderful returns. Looking back over my boyhood days, I praise God for the enrichment that came into my life through godly men and women who passed through our home. Impressions made in formative years stand a child in good stead in maturity.[9]

Helga Henry, the wife of the renowned theologian Carl F. H. Henry, reminds us that "Christian hospitality is not a matter of choice; it is not a matter of money; it is not a matter of age, social standing, sex, or personality. Christian hospitality is a matter of obedience to God."[10]

Notes to Chapter 11

1. An excellent article to read and make available to your church is "A Friendly Church Is Hard to Find," by Gene and Nancy Preston in *Christian Century* (Jan. 30, 1991), 102-03. Available online at *www.lewisandroth.org*.

2. Quoted in Thomas S. Gosin II, *The Church without Walls* (Pasadena, Calif.: Hope, 1984), 68.

3. *Conversations with Luther: Table Talk*, trans. and ed. Preserved Smith and Herbert Percival Gallinger (New Canaan, Conn.: Keats Publishing Inc., 1979), xii.

4. T. E. Koshy, *Brother Bakht Singh of India* (Secunderabad, India: OM Books, 2003), 102.

5. Ibid., 91.

6. Michael Green, *Evangelism in the Early Church* (Grand Rapids, Mich.: Eerdmans, 1970), 207.

7. Ibid., 223.

8. Jim Petersen, *Evangelism as a Lifestyle* (Colorado Springs: NavPress, 1980), 96-97.

9. Stephen F. Olford, "Christian Hospitality," *Decision* (March 1968), 10.

10. Quoted from V. A. Hall, *Be My Guest* (Chicago: Moody Press, 1979), 9.

Chapter 12

Caring for Peoples' Needs

Did not I weep for him whose day was hard?
Was not my soul grieved for the needy?
Job 30:25

Compassion is the empathy, the tender emotion a person feels when confronted with another person's suffering, coupled with the desire to relieve the suffering. Such a formal definition, however, doesn't do much to inspire action. So Jesus, the master teacher, explains compassionate love with the unforgettable story of the Good Samaritan (Luke 10:30-37).

A man was traveling from Jerusalem to Jericho when he was robbed. The robbers stole his money, stripped him of his clothes, and brutally beat him. As he lay bleeding to death, a Jewish priest (a religious leader and teacher of the people) passed by. The priest saw the injured man but continued on his way. Shortly after, a Jewish Levite (an assistant to the priests) came along. He too saw the helpless man but did nothing.

Finally, a man from Samaria passed by. Although the Samaritan traveler didn't know the victim, we are told that "he had compassion" (Luke 10: 33). He stopped and cared for the victim, pouring oil and wine over the wounds and tenderly bandaging them, then he lifted the man up onto his animal and took him to an inn. The next day the Samaritan had to leave, so he gave the innkeeper money for the injured man's food and lodging and asked the innkeeper to care for him.

The Good Samaritan also promised to return and pay any additional costs incurred while the man recuperated. He did all this for a man he didn't know, and he did it without any promise of reward.

This story sets the standard for Christian love and compassion. When we grasp the implications of the Good Samaritan we'll understand what

A leader will not have much of a ministry if people do not know that he or she truly cares about them.

our Lord requires of those who profess to love as he loved. Think of the religious priest and Levite who walked by the dying man and did nothing. They were religious leaders and teachers, so they knew the Old Testament demands "love your neighbor as yourself" (Lev. 19:18). But they were men who lacked compassion. If we want to be loving Christian leaders, we must be as selfless and compassionate as the Good Samaritan.

Compassionate New Testament Leaders

The word that jumps out of the gospels describing Jesus' emotion toward people in need is *compassion*.[1] Our Lord often felt compassion, or was moved with compassion to heal and to save. The compassionate care he and the apostles gave to the poor and the sick is inspirational. His "unheard-of acts of compassion" drew people to him like a magnet.[2]

After Jesus Christ ascended into heaven, the apostles were involved in compassionate ministry to the poor believers in Jerusalem (Acts 4:34-35). In fact, their work of distributing money to the poor became so burdensome that they had to appoint seven men to take over this task so that they could concentrate on prayer and the ministry of the word (Acts 6:1-6).

Although Paul's primary calling was the proclamation and defense of the gospel, he also gladly cared for the needy (Acts 11:30; Gal. 2:10). At one point in his ministry Paul initiated, mobilized, and delivered a Gentile relief offering for the poor believers in Jerusalem. He considered the giving by the Gentile churches to be a concrete demonstration of Christian love to the needy Jewish believers (2 Cor. 8:24).[3]

The New Testament elders' ministry involves pastoral oversight of the local church in four major categories: teaching, leading, protecting, and healing.[4] Although elders teach and lead the church, they also minister to the weak and sick (Acts 20:34-35; Titus 1:8; James 5:14). Thus they are to have a heart of compassion for the needs of people. The New Testament deacons' ministry is one of benevolence, mercy, and servanthood in an official capacity.[5] Both elders and deacons, then, are to demonstrate loving compassion and proactive concern for the welfare of needy saints. They are to set an example for others to follow.

Leaders Model Compassionate Care

The local church is to be a family, a community of people who meet one another's needs, bear one another's burdens, and sacrificially serve one another. It is to be a picture of love in action—a compassionate, generous, and giving community.[6] Such love starts with the leaders.

It's true that people don't care how much you know until they know how much you care. A leader will not have much of a ministry if people do not know that he or she truly cares about them. So a leader needs to demonstrate a tender heart toward suffering members, a genuine concern for the sick, a generous disposition to the poor, and a spirit of mercy to help relieve the misery that characterizes the lives of so many people today.

Compassion for the Sick

In a world full of physical pain and sickness, loving concern is an essential ministry of those who desire or claim to express God's love on earth. Compassionate care for the sick includes prayer, visits, practical helps, calls, notes, and cards.

Prayer is a very meaningful expression of concern. We should never say apologetically, "Well, all I can do is pray for you." Such a remark suggests a low view of prayer. God says, "Confess your sins to one another and pray for one another, that you may be healed. The effective prayer of a righteous person has great power" (James 5:16). In reality, praying for those who are sick or dying is one of the most important things we can do for them. Prayer gives

> A leader needs to demonstrate a tender heart toward suffering members, a genuine concern for the sick, a generous disposition to the poor, and a spirit of mercy.

hope and comfort. So in faith, leaders should regularly pray for the sick, and we should challenge our congregations to engage in focused, consistent, personal prayer for them as well.

People who are sick need not only prayer but also human touch. It is both healing and comforting. A sick person longs for compassion and companionship. Sometimes a sick person, particularly someone who is facing death, just needs to know that someone is near. When we visit the sick or dying, we are ministering God's love and comfort. This is a great privilege and a high calling. Jesus touched the lepers and the blind, the "untouchables" of his day, and he expects his people to do the same (Matt. 25:36).

In reality, when acts of love become time-consuming or demanding, we don't want the burdens of love—just the benefits.

Sadly, people are reluctant to visit the sick or the shut-ins. Taking time to visit them at home or in the hospital has become an inconvenience to many in our highly individualistic, hyperactive society. We may want to think of ourselves as loving people, but in reality, when acts of love become time-consuming or demanding, we don't want the burdens of love—just the benefits.

> We are willing to love up to the point where it begins to be inconvenient to love any more. We like the image of ourselves as loved and loving people, but we would like the benefit without the responsibilities of the role. When the response to our love presents us with demands, we may begin to hold people off.[7]

The love of Christ, however, constrains us to deny ourselves in order to meet the needs of others. We may not be able to visit everyone we would like, but we can call on the phone. The phone is an invaluable tool that we should use effectively to encourage and check on those who are suffering. People appreciate a thoughtful phone call. They know we can't visit every day, and sometimes a visit isn't appropriate, but we can call. Loving leaders find themselves making lots of phone calls.

People who are sick also appreciate cards, e-mails, and letters. A man in our church who was dying of cancer so appreciated the cards people sent that he filled an entire wall with the cards he received. He read them many times and viewed each one as a personal message of love. The cards on that wall provided daily affirmation that he was cared about and prayed for by a number of people. This visible means of encouragement strengthened his spirit.

Some of the best medicine for the sick and dying is practical, loving care. They may need help with meals, housecleaning, or rides to the doctor's office. When we help people in these ways, we demonstrate love and care for the body of Christ (Matt. 25:35-36).

Compassion for Shut-ins and the Elderly

We must all be aware of and look out for the growing senior population. Some have called elderly people without any family support "senior orphans." Christian compassion cannot allow them to be neglected. We must honor the elderly.

Shut-ins and the elderly are a group easily forgotten or overlooked. Because of physical or mental disability, they may suffer loneliness and isolation from friends. They may be unable to attend church. They need phone calls, cards, visits, church bulletins, recorded messages, and the Lord's Supper to keep them connected with their church family. If these

John warns against love that is merely lip-service, talk, or theory.

loving acts are neglected, they will feel abandoned. James writes, "Religion that is pure and undefiled before God, the Father, is this: to visit orphans and widows in their affliction" (James 1:27). Shut-ins experience various types of "affliction" and need our compassionate love.

Compassion for the Poor and Needy

John describes the standard of love among believers envisioned by the New Testament:

> By this we know love, that he laid down his life for us, and we ought to lay down our lives for the brothers. But if anyone has the world's goods and sees his brother in need, yet closes his heart against him, how does God's love abide in him? Little children, let us not love in word or talk but in deed and in truth. (1 John 3:16-18)

Here John warns against love that is merely lip-service, talk, or theory. In contrast to this so-called love that refuses to show compassion, he describes a love that expresses itself not only in word but in deed. Christian love is never theoretical or abstract; it is always practical. The one who loves is compelled to act in order to relieve the suffering of the one who is loved.

Elaborating on John's declaration, Leon Morris writes:

> But John is practical. He knows that a man may easily declare himself ready to lay down his life for others, because words are cheap, and such a sacrifice is unlikely to be required. What he demands is not this heroic gesture, but a daily sharing of what one has with those who have not. Taking thought for the day-to-day needs of people in want is a duty John sees as a necessary consequence of the cross. The cross shows us what *agape* is: a readiness not only to die for others but to live for others. Love is not a fragile treasure to be tucked away securely somewhere; it is a robust virtue to be practiced in everyday life.[8]

Jonathan Edwards reminds us that the nature of love is to "dispose men to all acts of mercy toward their neighbours.... It will dispose men to give to the poor, to bear one another's burdens, and to weep with those that weep."[9] The first Christian congregation and its leaders organized itself to care for its poor members (Acts 4:34-35; 6:1-6). When writing about brotherly love, Paul exhorted the Christians at Rome to "contribute to the needs of the saints" (Rom. 12:13).

To have the means to help a fellow believer in need but to refuse is disobedience to Christ and sin against the body of Christ. This type of behavior raises the question of whether God's love dwells in such a heart.

We all need examples of loving, compassionate leaders. One such leader was Job. An elder in his community,[10] he was "blameless and upright" (Job 1:1), a man who showed compassion for the poor and needy. Job had a tender heart for those who suffered. He wept and grieved for the brokenhearted. He responded with generous assistance to the cries of the poor, the orphan, the widow, and the disabled. Job was also a man of large-hearted hospitality.

To his cold-hearted, know-it-all friends, themselves elders in the community, he spoke in his own defense:

> Did not I weep for him whose day was hard?
> Was not my soul grieved for the needy? (Job 30:25)

Because I delivered the poor who cried for help,
and the fatherless who had none to help him.
The blessing of him who was about to perish came upon me,
and I caused the widow's heart to sing for joy.
I put on righteousness, and it clothed me;
my justice was like a robe and a turban.
I was eyes to the blind and feet to the lame.
I was a father to the needy, and I searched out
the cause of him who I did not know. (Job 29:12-16)

If I have witheld anything that the poor desired,
or have caused the eyes of the widow to fail,
or have eaten my morsel alone,
and the fatherless has not eaten of it ...
if I have seen anyone perish for lack of clothing,
or the needy without covering ...
then let my shoulder blade fall from my shoulder,
and my arm be broken from its socket. (Job 31:16-17, 19, 22)

Today we can demonstrate compassion by providing free counseling for elderly widows and widowers to help them understand tax questions, medical insurance papers, and wills. We can invite them to our home for food and fellowship. We can provide signing translation for the deaf who come to our church. We can furnish transportation for the blind and invite them to our homes for hospitality. We can organize a benevolence fund for those who have lost their jobs, for the disabled, or for single mothers raising young children. We can establish a program for boys and girls without fathers. We can see to it that people with disabilities feel welcome and safe in our churches and homes. We can provide language training for new immigrants.

Leaders and teachers can cast a vision and set an example of compassionate care.

As leaders and teachers, we can make a difference. We can cast a vision and set an example of compassionate care. We can raise awareness and set up organizational structures providing opportunities for people to share with others in need. We can also warn of how materialism, prosperity, and greed harden the heart and blind our eyes to the terrible suffering of our fellow believers as well as that of other human beings.

Our world is filled with poverty and sickness. Almost 800 million people go to bed hungry every night. Almost three billion people (half the world's population) live on less than $2 a day. A billion people drink unsafe water; 2.5 billion people do not have safe sanitation. More than ten million children under the age of five years die each year of preventable causes. Seventy percent of the world's poor are women and children. Every day, 27,000 children die from hunger and related causes. More than a million young girls are forced into prostitution each year.

And the suffering in our world doesn't end with these problems. "The biggest public health problem the world has ever faced," according to Dale Bourke, is the present AIDS crisis.[11] This pandemic claims the lives of 8,500 people every day. Bourke writes,

> It has already surpassed the bubonic plague, which wiped out twenty-five million people—one quarter of Europe's population at the time. An estimated three million people die each year from AIDS, a death toll that has been compared to twenty fully loaded 747s crashing every single day for a year.
>
> AIDS has now spread to every country in the world.... Reported AIDS cases are rising so swiftly in China and India that they could eventually eclipse the numbers in Africa.... In some countries more than one-third of the population is infected, effectively wiping out an entire generation."[12]

The suffering in Africa as a result of AIDS, continual wars, and famine is beyond our comprehension. Do we care? What can we do to help?

A Greek scholar who participated on a committee for producing a new Bible translation was also an active board member of an organization to feed the poor. He was asked, "Doesn't it seem strange that you serve on one committee to translate the Bible and on another to feed the poor?"

"No," he replied. "In both ways I am translating the New Testament."

Notes to Chapter 12

1. Matt. 9:13, 36; 12:7; 14:14; 15:32; 20:34; Mark 1:41; 6:34; 8:2; Luke 7:13.

2. William L. Lane, *Commentary on the Gospel of Mark*, NICNT (Grand Rapids, Mich.: Eerdmans, 1974), 87.

3. Acts 24:17; Rom. 15:25-28; 1 Cor. 16:1-3; 2 Cor. 8–9.

4. Acts 15:6-29; 20:17; 28-31; 1 Tim. 5:17-18; Titus 1:9; 1 Peter 5:1-4. See Alexander Strauch, *Biblical Eldership: An Urgent Call to Restore Biblical Church Leadership* (Littleton, Colo.: Lewis & Roth, 1995).

5. See Alexander Strauch, *The New Testament Deacon: The Church's Ministry of Mercy* (Littleton, Colo.: Lewis & Roth, 1992).

6. Acts 2:45; 4:32–5:11; 9:36; Rom. 12:13; 15:25-27; 2 Cor. 8–9; Gal. 2:9-10; Eph. 4:28; 1 Tim. 5:9-10; 6:17-19; Heb. 13:16; James 1:27, 2:14-15.

7. Reuel L. Howe, *Herein Is Love* (Chicago: Judson, 1965), 33.

8. Leon Morris, *Testaments of Love* (Grand Rapids, Mich.: Eerdmans, 1981), 179.

9. Jonathan Edwards, *Charity and Its Fruits* (1852; reprint ed., Edinburgh: Banner of Truth, 1978), 8.

10. Job 29:7, 21, 25; 31:21.

11. Dale Hanson Bourke, *The Skeptic's Guide to the Global AIDS Crisis* (Waynesboro, Ga.: Authentic Media, 2004), 5. This edition updated in 2005. For more statistics on AIDS see *www.who.org* and *www.unaids.org*.

12. Ibid., 5.

Chapter 13

Laboring in Prayer

*Epaphras greets you, always struggling
on your behalf in his prayers.*
Col. 4:12

Loving leadership is incomplete without intercessory prayer. The Scripture says, "Let love be genuine," and then goes on to say, "be constant in prayer" (Rom. 12:9, 12). Praying for people is an act of love. Genuine love desires to pray for people. Hypocritical love promises to pray but doesn't.

Prayer requires effort. When we pray for people, we focus our thoughts on them; we take their burdens upon ourselves; we intercede before God for them; we sacrifice our time for them; we commit ourselves to their well-being. We demonstrate true care and compassion.

Martyn Lloyd-Jones reminds us that prayer can be one of the most difficult things we do in the Christian life:

> When a man is speaking to God he is at his very acme. It is the highest activity of the human soul, and therefore it is at the same time the ultimate test of a man's true spiritual condition. There is nothing that tells the truth about us as Christian people so much as our prayer life. Everything we do in the Christian life is easier than prayer.[1]

Difficult though it may be, prayer is motivated by love. Paul's love for his converts, for example, drove him to pray for them continually.[2] D. A. Carson says what motivated Paul to pray was "a passion for people."[3] Describing Paul's love for the new believers at Thessalonica, he writes:

117

Here is a Christian so committed to the well-being of other Christians, especially new Christians, that he is simply burning up inside to be with them, to help them, to nurture them, to feed them, to stabilize them, to establish an adequate foundation for them. Small wonder, then, that he devotes himself to praying for them when he finds he cannot visit them personally.[4]

Carson summarizes Paul's motivation and challenges us to grow in love that overflows in intercessory prayer for others:

Paul's prayer is the product of his passion for people. His unaffected fervency in prayer is not whipped-up emotionalism but the overflow of his love for brothers and sisters in Christ Jesus.

That means that if we are to improve our praying, we must strengthen our loving. As we grow in disciplined, self-sacrificing love, so we will grow in intercessory prayer. Superficially fervent prayers devoid of such love are finally phony, hollow, shallow.[5]

Paul is an example of a loving leader who labored in prayer. Compelled to pray not only for the saved but also for the lost, he burned with love for Israel and prayed for her salvation: "Brothers, my heart's desire and prayer to God for them is that they may be saved" (Rom.10:1). Christian leaders likewise need to pray for the lost.

Paul's companion Epaphras is another inspiring example of a loving leader who fervently prayed for those he loved. While Epaphras was with Paul in the city of Rome, Paul wrote to the church in Colossae and told them about the prayers of Epaphras on their behalf:

Epaphras … greets you, always struggling on your behalf in his prayers, that you may stand mature and fully assured in all the will of God. For I bear him witness that he has worked hard for you and for those in Laodicea and in Hierapolis. (Col. 4:12-13)

Note that Epaphras was "always struggling" in prayer for his beloved people. Other translations render the phrase this way: "He is continually wrestling in prayer for you,"[6] he "never stops battling for you" in prayer (NJB). "It was not an occasional, listless prayer on their behalf," comments D. Edmond

Hiebert, "but a constant burden of intercession. Regularly and repeatedly he bore them up before the throne of grace."[7]

How blessed the believers in Colossae were to have such a faithful, loving shepherd. The intercessory prayers of Ephaphras for his countrymen flowed out of his love for them and followed in the footsteps of his mentor, who constantly prayed for all those under his pastoral care. As H. C. G. Moule states, "Epaphras was Paul's true scholar in the school of intercession."[8]

How to Get Started

While spontaneous prayer has its place in our lives, there is also a need for disciplined, intercessory prayer. Paul appeals to the believers in Rome to actively *wrestle* in prayer to God for his safety and travel: "I appeal to you … by the love of the Spirit, to strive together with me in your prayers to God on my behalf" (Rom. 15:30). Notice that Paul appeals to them for prayer "by the love of the Spirit." If they love

> **"There is nothing that tells the truth about us as Christian people so much as our prayer life."**
>
> **—D. Martyn Lloyd-Jones**

him, they will pray for him. But this love is not some short-lived, sentimental feeling for a missionary. This love is the love produced by God the Holy Spirit. The Spirit is the source of this love. It is the love that all believers should have for one another. The "love of the Spirit" would thus be the power that moves them to "strive" in disciplined intercessory prayer for the needs of a person they love.

Disciplined prayer is a particularly urgent challenge today, for the busyness of life leaves little time for it unless we make it a priority and plan for it. It is all too common for leaders to neglect the patient ministry of prayer both for and with others. George Verwer, founder of Operation Mobilization, observes,

> But if there is any doctrine to which we pay only lip service in our churches, it has to be the doctrine of prayer. I have ministered in thousands of churches … in Europe, North America, and around the world and I have never ceased to be amazed at the neglect of true, heart-felt, corporate prayer. There are some beautiful exceptions, of course, but they are few by comparison.[9]

D. A. Carson concurs and adds that prayerlessness "is out of step with the Bible that portrays what Christian living should be":

> What is both surprising and depressing is the sheer prayerlessness that characterizes so much of the Western church. It is surprising, because it is out of step with the Bible that portrays what Christian living should be; it is depressing, because it frequently coexists with abounding Christian activity that somehow seems hollow, frivolous, and superficial.[10]

Lack of intercessory prayer is not only a sign of lovelessness, it is an indication of our failure to see the dark spiritual realities surrounding us. Prayer is critical because we are at war "against the cosmic powers over this present darkness, against the spiritual forces of evil in the heavenly places." So we must "take up the full armor of God" (Eph. 6:12-13) and, being fully armored, persevere in Spirit-empowered prayer:

> praying at all times in the Spirit, with all prayer and supplication. To that end keep alert with all perseverance, making supplication for all the saints, and also for me, that words may be given to me in opening my mouth boldly to proclaim the mystery of the gospel. (Eph. 6:18-19)

Let us not be prayerless leaders, but let us be vigilant. Paul and Epaphras were "alert" soldiers of Jesus Christ. They both prayed "for all the saints," "at all times," and "with all perseverance." We likewise must be alert and pray for all the saints under our care. Failure to pray is serious negligence of both our privilege and our responsibility as leaders, teachers, and ministers of the gospel. The prophet Samuel considered prayerlessness on the part of a leader of God's people to be sin: "Far be it from me that I should sin against the Lord by ceasing to pray for you" (1 Sam. 12:23).

> **"Prayerlessness ... frequently coexists with abounding Christian activity that somehow seems hollow, frivolous, and superficial."**
> **—D. A. Carson**

In every congregation, spiritual problems and physical needs exist for which the only solution is believing, persistent prayer. There are those suffering daily physical pain, some facing life-threatening illness, others dealing with heartbreaking family problems. Many need prayer because they struggle with addictions or sins that are enslaving them and ruining their relationships. Some are not yet saved and need salvation.

When confronted with a problem that his disciples could not resolve, a boy tormented by an evil spirit, our Lord said, "This kind cannot be driven out by anything but prayer" (Mark 9:29). Thus we

Samuel considered prayerlessness on the part of a leader of God's people to be sin.

must believe that "the prayer of a righteous person has great power as it is working" (James 5:16) or we will not put forth the effort to labor in prayer for the needs of others.

The best teachers and preachers labor to improve their teaching skills, and they should. Competent leaders and administrators seek to continually improve their leadership abilities, and they should. So, too, believer priests should labor to improve their intercessory prayer ministry. Below are a few suggestions to help you begin praying for those you teach and lead.

Information

To pray intelligently, we need information; we need current prayer requests. Hudson Taylor, a missionary with extensive experience in striving in prayer for hundreds of missionaries in the most trying situations conceivable, taught that information from missionaries was vital to keeping prayer alive on the home front. A. J. Broomhall, Taylor's biographer, writes,

> When Christians knew what was going on they rose to the occasion and joined in. When feeling out of touch, their gifts and even praying seemed to dwindle. Information led to dedication—of their whole lives in many instances.[11]

As a loving leader, make a deliberate effort to learn the heart-felt needs of those you lead and teach. Don't assume you know their problems and concerns. Ask! Love cares and wants to know. This will stir your heart to pray and help energize your prayers. Let people know you pray for them and need their prayer requests. But because many people are reluctant to talk about their real needs, you will need to be the one to take the initiative.

Finally, do not tell people you will pray for them and then fail to do it. That is hypocritical love. Genuine love takes the promises of prayer to heart and follows through in keeping those promises.

Prayer List

To labor effectively in intercessory prayer for others, you will need to develop a prayer list of names and needs. Since most of us don't have a photographic memory, we need to write down prayer requests. If you are among those responsible for the whole congregation, you will be praying for many people and needs. To do this effectively, use the church directory of names to conscientiously and systematically pray "for all the saints" (Eph. 6:18). Pray for your missionaries as well (Eph. 6:19-20). And don't forget to put your enemies on a prayer list too. Jesus says to love your enemies by praying for them (Matt. 5:44; Luke 6:28). D. A. Carson aptly observes, "All of us would be wiser if we would resolve never to put people down, except on our prayer lists."[12]

Biblical Prayer

If at times you don't know how to pray for those you lead, look in your Bible. It is the very best prayer guide. You can use the prayers of Scripture in praying for others (and yourself). Here are some examples:

+ O LORD God of heaven, the great and awesome God who keeps covenant and steadfast love ... I now pray before you day and night for the people of Israel your servants, confessing the sins of the people of Israel, which we have sinned against you. Even I and my father's house have sinned. We have acted very corruptly against you and have not kept the commandments, the statutes, and the rules that you commanded your servant Moses. (Neh. 1:5-8)

+ I am praying for them ... they are yours ... Holy Father.... I do not ask that you take them out of the world, but that you keep them from the evil one.... Sanctify them in the truth; your word is truth ... that they may become perfectly one, so that the world may know that you sent me. (John 17:9, 11, 15, 17, 23)

- Remembering you in my prayers, that the God of our Lord Jesus Christ, the Father of glory, may give you a spirit of wisdom and of revelation in the knowledge of him, having the eyes of your hearts enlightened, that you may know what is the hope to which he has called you, what are the riches of his glorious inheritance in the saints, and what is the immeasurable greatness of his power toward us who believe. (Eph. 1:16-19)

- It is my prayer that your love may abound more and more, with knowledge and all discernment, so that you may approve what is excellent, and so be pure and blameless for the day of Christ, filled with the fruit of righteousness that comes through Jesus Christ, to the glory and praise of God. (Phil. 1:9-11)

- We have not ceased to pray for you, asking that you may be filled with the knowledge of his will in all spiritual wisdom and understanding, so as to walk in a manner worthy of the Lord, fully pleasing to him, bearing fruit in every good work and increasing in the knowledge of God. (Col. 1:9-10)

- To this end we always pray for you, that our God may make you worthy of his calling and may fulfill every resolve for good and every work of faith by his power, so that the name of our Lord Jesus may be glorified in you, and you in him. (2 Thess. 1:11-12)

- May the Lord make you increase and abound in love for one another and for all ... so that he may establish your hearts blameless in holiness before our God and Father, at the coming of our Lord Jesus with all his saints. (1 Thess. 3:12-13)

You can take these very words and apply them to the people you are praying for. This will give your prayers a solid, scriptural foundation. You will be confident that you are praying the will of God for others and you will know what God wants for them. Praying the words of Scripture puts life in your prayers.

Out of love for those you lead, commit yourself to improving your intercessory prayer. Ask yourself, *If those I lead were dependent on my prayers, how would they do?* Or, *If our missionaries were dependent on my prayers, how would they do?*

To strengthen your prayer life, take your Bible concordance and look up all the verses on prayer to see what God wants you to know about prayer. Read books on prayer and talk to others to get practical ideas. Pray with mature believers, and learn from hearing them. Make a prayer list of those for whom you will pray regularly and set aside a place and time to do it. Even five or ten minutes a day of faithful prayer for those under your care will yield great benefits. Some prayer is better than no prayer. As you practice the discipline of prayer and see many marvelous answers from the Lord, and as you grow in love, you will become more devoted to prayer.

Like the disciples, we can ask our Lord to teach us to pray (Luke 11:1), and then faithfully obey the commands of Scripture to pray at all times, with perseverance, for all the saints (Eph. 6:18).

Notes to Chapter 13

1. D. Martyn Lloyd-Jones, *Studies in the Sermon on the Mount,* 2 vols. (Grand Rapids, Mich.: Eerdmans, 1971), 2:46.
2. Rom. 1:9-10; 2 Cor. 13:7, 9; Eph. 1:16; Phil. 1:3-4; Col. 1:3, 9; 1 Thess. 1:2; 3:10; 2 Thess. 1:11.
3. D. A. Carson, *A Call to Spiritual Reformation: Priorities from Paul and His Prayers* (Grand Rapids, Mich.: Baker, 1992), 79.
4. Ibid., 81.
5. Ibid., 85.
6. F. F. Bruce, *The Letters of Paul: An Expanded Paraphrase* (Grand Rapids, Mich.: Eerdmans, 1965), 259.
7. D. Edmond Hiebert, "Epaphras, Man of Prayer," *Bibliotheca Sacra* 136 (January-March 1979): 59.
8. H. C. G. Moule, *The Epistles of Paul the Apostle to the Colossians and to Philemon,* CBSC (Cambridge: University Press, 1906), 141.
9. George Verwer, "Whatever Happened to the Prayer Meeting?" *SurgeUp* (*www.thinkwow.com/surgeup/whatever_happened.htm.* Accessed Oct. 3, 2005).
10. Carson, *A Call to Spiritual Reformation,* 9.
11. A.J. Broomhall, *Hudson Taylor and China's Open Century,* vol. 5: *Refiner's Fire* (London: Hodder and Stoughton, 1985), 342.
12. Carson, *A Call to Spiritual Reformation,* 29.

Chapter 14

Feeding Hungry Souls

Do you love me? ... Feed my sheep.
John 21:17

Good shepherds love their sheep and spare no effort when leading them to green pastures and clear water. For the lazy shepherd, however, any pasture or water hole will do. In the Old Testament, God has strong words for lazy shepherds. In Ezekiel, God condemned Israel's leaders for neglecting to feed his people (Ezek. 34:2). In Hosea, the priests failed to teach God's law thus God cried out, "My people are destroyed for lack of knowledge" (Hos. 4:6). But someday, God promises Israel, "I will give you shepherds after my own heart, who will feed you with knowledge and understanding" (Jer. 3:15).

Jesus Christ is the Good Shepherd—a shepherd after God's own heart who poured out his life feeding people the Word of God. Thus they called him "Teacher." Even now, from heaven, Jesus Christ gives spiritual gifts to enable some to feed his flock (Eph. 4:11-16). Because he loves his people, he wants them to have his nourishing words, "the words of life" (John 6: 63, 68), so they can grow to maturity and reproduce themselves. Loving leaders and teachers likewise will devote their lives to feeding God's flock.

Love Teaches and Strengthens

When we see pictures of emaciated, starving children our hearts grieve and we want to help. So, too, our hearts should grieve when we see God's people emaciated and starving spiritually because of a famine of the Word of God.

We should want to take immediate action because *love always seeks to provide loved ones' needs and the greatest need people have is for the Word of God.* The Lord himself says: "Man does not live by bread alone, but man lives by every word that comes from the mouth of the Lord" (Deut. 8:3). The Word of God provides the message of eternal salvation and the guidelines for the Christian life (2 Tim. 3:15-17).

Love for people compels us to preach and teach God's Word. It empowers us to exhaust ourselves in reading, study, and preparation for teaching. It inspires us to sacrifice significant amounts of time in teaching one-on-one, or in small groups, or in full congregational meetings. It

Love cannot bear to see loved ones in spiritual poverty, starving for the Word of God, and it will not leave them in ignorance.

gives us the desire to educate all people, young and old, educated and uneducated. Love cannot bear to see loved ones in spiritual poverty, starving for the Word of God, and it will not leave them in ignorance.

God's people need spiritual food and nourishment to grow and reproduce. This is why Paul tells Timothy to make the teaching of Scripture central to his ministry: "Devote yourself to the public reading of Scripture, to exhortation, to teaching [based on Scripture]" (1 Tim. 4:13). Commentator William Mounce accurately states, "Leadership in the apostolic church was largely based on proper teaching."[1]

Barnabas is a wonderful example of a loving leader with a passion for building others up through the Scripture. The first Christians called him "son of exhortation" (Acts 4:36). By the Word of the Lord, Barnabas lifted people's spirits. He strengthened and challenged their faith. He inspired fresh courage and commitment to Christ (Acts 11:23). He educated new believers in Christ (Acts 11:26; 13:1). His love for teaching the gospel drove him to seek out Paul in the city of Tarsus and bring him to Antioch so the new church there would have the best instruction possible. Together, Paul and Barnabas could teach the Word and build a mature, healthy flock.

A modern day Barnabas is Robert Chapman, who left his legal profession to become pastor of a small, troubled, Baptist congregation in Barnstaple, England. Despite his excellent skills with people, shepherding the church in Barnstaple would prove to be a challenging task. To start with, he had to overcome potentially explosive doctrinal differences between himself and the congregation.

It is remarkable that Ebenezer Chapel invited him to become pastor, since he had never been a Baptist and did not share many of the church's strict views. Given the doctrinal tensions between Robert Chapman and the church, the situation at Ebenezer seemed doomed to failure. He was likely to be the fourth pastor to leave in less than two years.

But that did not happen. Robert Chapman firmly believed that unless he had the liberty to teach God's Word, there could be no ministry for him at Ebenezer Chapel. So he wisely laid down one nonnegotiable condition before accepting the pastorate at Ebenezer. That condition is best explained by Chapman himself:

When I was invited to leave London and go to minister the Word of God in Ebenezer Chapel, then occupied by a community of Strict Baptists, I consented to do so, naming one condition only—that I should be free to teach all I found written in the Scriptures.[2]

To their credit, the people agreed to this condition and Robert Chapman began his sixty-year ministry in Barnstaple. Gradually the church changed under his straightforward, consistent Bible teaching. As the years passed, it became a mature, influential congregation of believers, planting many churches and having a broad mission outreach to Spain, India, and China.

> "Leadership in the apostolic church was largely based on proper teaching."
> —William Mounce

Love demands that we meet people's basic need to hear the Word of God (Deut. 8:3). What a colossal failure it is for church shepherds to do everything but feed God's flock. The Bible is the believers' food. Continual nourishment through the milk and the meat of God's Word is what they need for protection and growth. Loving leaders and teachers will labor diligently to meet that need.

Love Makes Teachers More Effective

Love not only motivates leaders to teach, it makes them more effective in their teaching. Good teachers need a caring rapport with their students, a loving character and personality, and a passion for their subject.

A Love for Students

Howard Hendricks, professor of Christian education at Dallas Seminary and popular speaker, has taught thousands of people how to improve their teaching. He tells this story of his Sunday school teacher, Walt.

Walt loved kids and he loved the Word of God. In a tough, inner-city environment, he walked the streets looking for unchurched kids to invite to his Sunday school class. In time, Walt was taking thirteen neighborhood boys to his class. Most of these boys received Christ, and eleven of them eventually entered full-time Christian ministry. One of these was Howard Hendricks. Walt wasn't an intellectual giant, nor did he have a particularly engaging personality; so what was it about him that reached these boys and impacted them for eternity? Hendricks says, "Actually, I can't tell you much of what Walt said to us, but I can tell you everything about him … because he loved me for Christ's sake. He loved me more than my parents did."[3]

Good teachers love their students and give themselves unselfishly to their education. They care about their students. They respect and value them. They know and understand them. Loving teachers are dedicated to their students' education. Like Paul, they can say, "we were ready to share with you not only the gospel of God but also our own selves, because you had become very dear to us" (1 Thess. 2:8).

Evangelical educators concur that love and respect for students is essential to life-changing instruction:

> No substitute exists for a teacher's love for his or her students.… Teaching is far more than getting across content; it also calls for communicating a genuine personal interest in and love for each student.[4]

A Loving Disposition

Good teachers must connect with their students. To do this, they must be the kind of loving people described in 1 Corinthians 13:4-7. People respond positively to teachers who display the characteristics of Christlike love.

Humble. In college I had a Christian teacher who regularly boasted in class about his advanced knowledge and prestigious publications. He was intelligent and a good lecturer, but he was not a Christlike teacher. Rather, he was arrogant and boastful, his tone of voice was condescending, he was full of himself rather than the Holy Spirit, he was trying to impress rather than edify. He was "a noisy gong ... a clanging cymbal" (1 Cor. 13:1).

In contrast, the Lord Jesus Christ said, "learn from me, for I am gentle and lowly in heart, and you will find rest for your souls" (Matt. 11:29). Everyone who heard Jesus teach knew that he was not like other teachers. He spoke with absolute authority, yet humbly and graciously, without arrogance. As a result, people from every level of society were drawn to him: men and women, rich and poor, educated and uneducated, healthy and sick, religious and nonreligious; even the outcasts of society were welcomed and enjoyed hearing his gracious words.

Love makes us better teachers because it makes us humble and modest. Love makes us servants of our students, not rulers over them. Love is willing to accept correction, to change, to improve, and to admit mistakes. Love helps us to realize that we don't know it all. Like Paul, we must confess, "we know in part and we prophesy in part" and "now we see in a mirror dimly" (1 Cor. 13:9, 12).

Love requires that we guard ourselves against pride in the pulpit and in the classroom. "Pride repels, humility attracts.... Effectiveness in teaching calls for humility in attitude."[5] A humble spirit makes us better representatives of Jesus Christ and his doctrine and makes people more receptive to our teaching. As John Oman warns, "unless the pulpit is the place where you are the humblest in giving God's message, it is certain to be the place where you are vainest in giving your own."[6]

Patient and kind. In a survey of college students preparing to be teachers, the students listed "love for and patience with pupils" as two of the most important qualities of a good teacher.[7] Love enables teachers to be patient and kind (1 Cor. 13:4), to suffer long with difficult people – even opponents (2 Tim. 2:24-26), and to endure problem people, like the stubborn Corinthians. Loving teachers take pains to help those who are slow to learn. They seek to draw in those who are uninterested. They demonstrate care and understanding for the special needs of some.

The Bible is difficult for most people to understand and retain (2 Peter 3:15-16); thus teachers need extraordinary patience. Many of the great doctrines we believe and teach are learned only by years—indeed, a lifetime —of learning line upon line, precept upon precept (Isa. 28:10, 13). Furthermore, new people come to our churches or Bible studies with doctrinal deficiencies or errors. If we are not patient and kind in dealing with them, we will drive them off before we have the opportunity to teach them.

As teachers, we must reason with people and persuade them. If we speak with graciousness, patience, and kindness, we will be more likely to convince them of the truth. Dogmatic, harsh attitudes, on the other hand, will repel and alienate people and make our teaching ineffective and unfruitful (2 Peter 1:8).

Tender and compassionate. When Jesus saw the crowds, "he had compassion on them ... and began to teach them many things" (Mark 6:34). Loving teachers, like Paul, treat people with tenderness and compassion. Paul likened himself to "a nursing mother taking care of her own children" (1 Thess. 2:7).

Wilson Thomas Hogg, first president of Greenville College, comments on the importance of speaking the truth with tenderness and love:

> Tenderness will win hearts so hardened that nothing else can move them. Truth spoken in love goes directly to the heart of the hearer and calls forth a kind response.... It overcomes prejudice and hardness.... It melts and wins where the most logical argument, the most terrible warning, and the severest threatening would produce no more impression than the falling of dew upon a block of granite.[8]

The truth of Wilson Hogg's statement was brought home to me at my baptism. I invited a long-time friend to witness my baptism and to hear a missionary speaker. The speaker was an Irishman who had served many years in Angola, Africa. My friend was a hardened unbeliever who came only because I asked him. He had heard gospel sermons before, and I had talked to him many times about the gospel, without any response. But after hearing the missionary speak, he asked, "Who is this man? I have never heard such a gracious and sincere speaker. I would like to meet him." Such a reaction was completely out of character for my friend. What drew this disinterested sinner was that, like Jesus, the missionary was "gentle and lowly in heart" (Matt. 11:29).

Slow to anger. Love is not easily irritated or angered by disagreement or opposition (1 Cor. 13:5). Good teachers are approachable and easy to talk to; they are not irritable, defensive, or quick to argue with people who disagree.

How we teach can be just as important as what we teach. We must not lose our temper, scold our students, yell at them, or seek revenge because they offend us. If we do, we give the devil the opportunity to ruin our teaching ministry (Eph. 4:26-27). We hurt rather than help our students and we lose our credibility. Angry preachers and teachers generate fear and stifle the spirit of inquiry, especially in children and adolescents.

Gracious. Loving teachers and leaders are not rude or ill-mannered (1 Cor. 13:5). They do not shame people publicly, interrupt them, insult them, talk over them, or bully them. They don't abuse their authority or intimidate people. They are careful in their speech and mindful of proper dress and decorum, particularly with members of the opposite sex. They are tactful, courteous, and polite. They recognize the value of other people's time and effort.

Balancing truth and love. Being compassionate and tenderhearted does not mean compromising the truth. Never! The biblical balance always maintains truth *and* love. The two are not to be separated (1 Cor. 13:1-3; Eph. 4:14-16; 2 John 3). John Stott offers insightful observations on the correct balance:

> Some leaders are great champions of the truth and anxious to fight for it, but display little love. Others are great advocates of love, but have no equal commitment to truth, as Jesus and his apostles had. Truth is hard if it is not softened by love, and love is soft if it is not strengthened by the truth.[9]

Whether we are defending, proclaiming, instructing, or informally sharing divine truth with others, we must always wrap it in love. We must always speak "the truth in love" (Eph. 4:15). To Timothy, a true son in the faith, Paul writes, "Follow the pattern of the sound words that you have heard from me, in the faith and love that are in Christ Jesus" (2 Tim. 1:13). So we see that "Timothy's maintenance of orthodox teaching must be accompanied and backed up by a genuine Christian way of life involving faith in God and love to others,"[10] as Howard Marshall expounds.

> **"Truth is hard if it is not softened by love, and love is soft if it is not strengthened by the truth."**
>
> **—John Stott**

Love for Studying and Communicating God's Word

The "great and first commandment" (Matt. 22:38) is to love God with all our heart and soul and mind. This love for God produces love for the study of his Word and motivates us to improve our ability to communicate it. Love for God's Word sets the heart on fire to always keep studying.

Gaining proficiency in God's Word. Good teachers love their subject and continue to learn. John Stott writes, "There is no doubt that the best teachers in any field of knowledge are those who remain students all their lives."[11]

A remarkable example of a lifelong student of Scripture is a ninety-seven-year-old man who teaches our church's seniors. He still loves to read, study, and teach the Word. Whenever I am with him, he talks of the Scriptures and the commentators he has read. We must never think of ourselves as too old to learn or to grow.

Love for God and his Word makes us lifelong students and thirsty learners. With customary insight, Charles Spurgeon warns of the tragedy when a teacher loses the desire to learn and study:

> We have all great need of much hard study if our ministry is to be good for anything.... He who has ceased to learn has ceased to teach. He who no longer sows in the study will no more reap in the pulpit.[12]

Howard Hendricks warns simply: "If you stop growing today, you stop teaching tomorrow."[13]

Paul Stanley and Robert Clinton, in their book *Connecting: The Mentoring Relationships You Need to Succeed in Life,* say that one of the primary reasons many Christian leaders and teachers do not finish their lives for Christ effectively is that at some point they stop growing in knowledge and in love for Christ.

> We have observed that most people cease learning by the age of forty. By that we mean they no longer actively pursue knowledge, understanding, and experience that will enhance their capacity to grow and contribute to others. Most simply rest on what they already know. But those who finish well maintain a *positive learning attitude* all their lives.
>
> Many people, particularly leaders, plateau. They become satisfied with where they are and with what they know. This often occurs after

they attain enough to be comfortable or can maintain a relatively secure and predictable future. But this contradicts the biblical principle of stewardship.[14]

In light of this natural tendency, Paul's charge to Timothy, after telling him to devote himself to teaching, bears repeating:

Practice these things, devote yourself to them, so that all may see your progress. Keep a close watch on yourself and on the teaching. Persist in this, for by so doing you will save both yourself and your hearers. (1 Tim. 4:15-16)

When we lose our zeal for knowledge, we lose our zest for teaching. When we stop growing, we stop influencing others. When we're not excited about Scripture, we don't excite others. If we expect to challenge the hearts and minds of men and women of the next generation, our hearts and minds must be challenged also. We cannot influence people for God if we are not learning, changing, and growing. Teachers who love God and love to study his Word reproduce this love in others.

Growing in the ability to communicate effectively. Love for God's people and his Word compels us to continually improve our communication skills so we may more effectively deliver the truth. Howard Hendricks warns,

If you are going to bore people, don't bore them with the Gospel. Bore them with calculus, bore them with earth science, bore them with world history. But it is a sin to bore people with the Gospel.[15]

There are very few naturally great preachers and teachers. Most of us are average teachers who continually need to improve our teaching and preaching skills. Yet the temptation is to be satisfied with our current level of competence and fruitfulness. If we love people and the holy Scriptures, however, we will never want to stop striving for improvement.

John MacArthur Jr. has been teaching the Bible through various media to large audiences of people for nearly forty years. In all this time he has not grown stale but is more passionate and more skilled than when he began. Love for the Word of God and love for his listeners motivates his commitment to excellence.

How to Get Started

Sheep are nearly incapable of properly feeding and watering themselves. Without a shepherd, they would soon be without pasture and water and starve to death or die of thirst. So, as author and pastor Charles Jefferson reminds us,

> everything depends on the proper feeding of the sheep. Unless wisely fed they become emaciated and sick, and the wealth invested in them is squandered. When Ezekiel presents a picture of the bad shepherd, the first stroke of his brush is—"he does not feed the flock." [16]

Here are a few ideas to help you improve your teaching. First, if you are part of a leadership team responsible for leading and teaching people, *lay out a clear biblical philosophy of teaching and preaching the Scriptures.* Also, regularly evaluate your teaching ministry and plan for the future. Be sure the content of your teaching is biblical, challenging, applicable, and relevant to the people. Don't let it become haphazard or ineffective. Be able to say as Paul did, "I did not shrink from declaring to you the whole purpose of God" (Acts 20:27). The sheep will suffer if you neglect this essential duty.

Second, to improve your teaching, listen to the expository teaching of excellent preachers and teachers, and make their tapes or CDs available to others. This has helped me immensely in my personal walk with the Lord as well as in my preaching. As I listen to the world's greatest preachers, they enrich my soul and demonstrate how to apply the Word of God to people's lives. They help me think of ways to illustrate difficult concepts, to be relevant, to organize a passage of Scripture, and to deliver the material with spiritual power and vitality.

Regularly evaluate your teaching ministry and plan for the future.

Third, always be building a library of Bible study tools to help you study the Scriptures. Of course, the most important thing is to have a good Bible. This is your primary source for feeding God's people. You will also need a good concordance, Bible dictionaries, quality commentaries, and other resources. There are good software programs as well as an increasing number of Bible study tools available online at no cost. [17]

Fourth, there are many books and other materials available to help you improve your preaching and teaching. Call a seminary or Bible college and ask the professor of homiletics for suggestions. Use these materials and make them available to others in your church. If possible, take a course on homiletics. Even if you have been to Bible school or seminary, you never outgrow your need for fresh ideas on improving your delivery of the truth. Seeing their leaders and teachers grow is greatly encouraging to people and encourages them to grow too.

Fifth, listen to yourself. Even the best preachers unwittingly fall into bad habits. Listening to yourself on audiotape, or even better, watching a videotape can help you correct annoying habits that hinder communication. Don't worry that this practice might cause pride; it will definitely keep you humble! Even the best teachers need to improve their skills.

Sixth, have someone close to you evaluate your teaching and preaching. Don't let others in your audience know you are doing this, as it will distract them from listening to the content of your teaching. My wife has been one of my best critics, and it hasn't ruined our marriage yet.

Finally, teachers and preachers need to "abound in love" if they are to be fruitful in their work. Charles Spurgeon says:

> Assuredly, we must abound in love. It is a hard thing for some preachers to saturate and perfume their sermons with love; for their natures are hard, or cold, or coarse, or selfish. We are none of us all that we ought to be, but some are specially poverty-stricken in point of love. They do not "naturally care" for the souls of men, as Paul puts it. To all, but especially to the harder sort, I would say, Be doubly earnest as to holy charity, for without this you will be no more than sounding brass or a tinkling cymbal. Love is power. The Holy Spirit, for the most part, works by our affection. Love men to Christ; faith accomplishes much, but love is the actual instrument by which faith works out its desires in the Name of the Lord of love.
>
> And I am sure that, until we heartily love our work, and love the people with whom we are working, we shall not accomplish much.[18]

Notes to Chapter 14

1. William Mounce, *Pastoral Epistles*, WBC (Nashville: Thomas Nelson, 2000), 392.

2. Frank Holmes, *Brother Indeed* (London: Victory Press, 1956), 31.

3. Howard Hendricks, *Teaching to Change Lives* (Sisters, Ore.: Multnomah, 1987), xiii.

4. Roy B. Zuck, *Teaching as Jesus Taught* (Grand Rapids, Mich.: Baker, 1995), 84.

5. Ibid., 67.

6. John Wood Oman, *Concerning the Ministry* (New York: Harper, 1937), 44.

7. Roy B. Zuck, *Teaching as Paul Taught* (Grand Rapids, Mich.: Baker, 1998), 61.

8. Wilson T. Hogg, *A Hand-Book of Homiletics and Pastoral Theology* (Chicago: Free Methodist Publishing House, 1919), 342-43.

9. John R. W. Stott, *The Message of 1 & 2 Thessalonians* orig. published as *The Gospel and the End of Time* (Downers Grove, Ill.: InterVarsity, 1991), 70.

10. I. Howard Marshall, *The Pastoral Epistles*, ICC (Edinburgh: T & T Clark, 1999), 714.

11. John R. W. Stott, *Between Two Worlds: The Art of Preaching in the Twentieth Century* (Grand Rapids, Mich.: Eerdmans, 1982), 180.

12. Charles Haddon Spurgeon, *An All-Round Ministry* (1900; reprint ed., London: Banner of Truth Trust, 1960), 236.

13. Hendricks, *Teaching to Change Lives*, 17.

14. Paul D. Stanley and J. Robert Clinton, *Connecting: The Mentoring Relationships You Need to Succeed in Life* (Colorado Springs: NavPress, 1992), 222.

15. Quoted in Lawrence O. Richards and Gary J. Bredfeldt, *Creative Bible Teaching*, rev. ed. (Chicago: Moody Press, 1998), 218.

16. Charles Edward Jefferson, *The Minister as Shepherd* (1912; reprint ed., Fincastle, N.J: Scripture Truth, n.d.), 59-60.

17. Internet sites include *www.bible.org* (home of the NET Bible), *www.biblegateway.com*, *www.bibleplaces.com*, and *www.biblestudytools.net*. Software programs such as Logos and BibleWorks also offer many helpful features.

18. Spurgeon, *An All-Round Ministry*, 192-93.

Chapter 15

Protecting and Reproving Loved Ones

Those whom I love, I reprove....
Rev. 3:19

Imagine a father who claims to love his children but takes no action to stop them from becoming drug addicts or prostitutes. Or imagine seeing a brother in Christ walking alone heading straight toward quicksand, but you say nothing and walk away in silence. This isn't genuine love; it's apathy. It is not loving one's neighbor as oneself; it is not loving as Jesus loved. Yet this is what we are like when we refuse to correct a wayward believer, to reprove sinful behavior, or to warn others of false teachers.

The Bible says we all are like sheep; without the protection of a good shepherd we easily go astray. We need shepherds, at every level in the church, who will give their life to protect the flock from savage wolves and other dangers.

Jesus Confronted Wolves in Sheep's Clothing

As the Good Shepherd, Jesus repeatedly warned his flock about the deadly influence of false teachers. Many people, including Jesus' disciples, thought the Pharisees and scribes were true teachers of the law and pious men. But they were not. They were hungry wolves who devoured people. In their religious zeal, they went far beyond the Old Testament by instituting thousands of ceremonial rituals and manmade traditions that made life almost unbearable for the people. They exalted themselves and were filled with self-righteousness. Worst of all, they hindered people from really knowing and loving God.

So Jesus sternly warned his disciples: "Beware of false prophets, who come to you in sheep's clothing but inwardly are ravenous wolves. You will recognize them by their fruits" (Matt. 7:15-16). With perfect moral indignation, Jesus identified their pernicious doctrines and false piety, publicly exposing them for who they really were:

* But woe to you, scribes and Pharisees, hypocrites! For you shut the kingdom of heaven in people's faces. (Matt. 23:13)
* Woe to you, blind guides.... (Matt. 23:16)
* So you also outwardly appear righteous to others, but within you are full of hypocrisy and lawlessness. (Matt. 23:28)
* You serpents, you brood of vipers, how are you to escape being sentenced to hell? (Matt. 23:33)
* You have a fine way of rejecting the commandment of God in order to establish your own tradition ... thus making void the word of God by your tradition. (Mark 7:9, 13)
* Beware of the scribes ... who devour widows' houses and for a pretense make long prayers. (Luke 20:46-47)

Jesus tells his disciples that the Pharisees will receive "greater condemnation" as teachers who have misled and devoured the defenseless (Luke 20:46-47).

Jesus' thundering against the Pharisees and scribes doesn't sound very loving or tolerant, and some people cannot imagine Jesus displaying moral indignation or expressing strong condemnation. But that is because they misunderstand who Jesus Christ is. His denunciation of the Pharisees and scribes was the expression of God's just and righteous judgment on them. The God of the Bible is not only a God of love but also a God of holy wrath and judgment. Divine love can be both tender and severe (Rom. 11:22).

Jesus is not an uncaring, angry prophet. He weeps over Jerusalem's rejection of his tender invitation to come to him for salvation (Matt. 23:37; Luke 19:41). He grieves over the hardened unbelief of the people and their leaders. Jesus is God's true prophet and teacher who risks his life to warn of danger. He is the watchman on the city wall crying out to protect the city from invaders.[1] He is the courageous protector who drives off the wolf, the lion, or bear, for he loves his sheep. Jesus declares, "I am the good shepherd. The good shepherd lays down his life for the sheep" (John 10:11).

When church teachers and leaders refuse to warn the flock of false teachers, it is an outright dereliction of duty that will result in the flock being devoured (Acts 20:28-31). Imagine a shepherd who avoids protecting the flock from wolves because it is dangerous, unpleasant work. What a preposterous thought! There are, however, Bible-believing churches so overly concerned about offending anyone because of the desire to increase their numbers that they will not warn people about false teachers. They are willing to leave the sheep vulnerable and defenseless against the wiles of the enemy.

Jesus Rebuked His Disciples

At times it was necessary for Jesus to rebuke his disciples for their unbelief and lack of understanding.[2] But Jesus was not a cold, abusive tyrant; he was a loving Master, "full of grace and truth" (John 1:14). Jesus never denounced his true disciples as he did the false teachers of Israel.

Actually, Jesus is remarkably patient and kind with his slow-to-learn disciples. He washes their feet, serves them, and teaches them. He cares for them and loves them, even when they desert him during his hour of crisis. As John's gospel states: "having loved his own who were in the world, he loved them to the end" (John 13:1). And in the end he died for them.

A. B. Bruce, in his monumental work *The Training of the Twelve*, reminds us of how much the disciples had to unlearn and learn in less than three years. Only the most highly skilled teacher and leader as Jesus was could have accomplished what he did with the Twelve:

> But at the time of their call they were exceedingly ignorant, narrow-minded, superstitious, full of Jewish prejudices, misconceptions, and animosities. They had much to unlearn of what was bad, as well as much to learn of what was good, and they were slow both to learn and to unlearn. Old beliefs already in possession of their minds made the communication of new religious ideas a difficult task. Men of good honest heart, the soil of their spiritual nature was fitted to produce an abundant harvest; but it was stiff, and needed much laborious tillage before it would yield its fruit.[3]

We, too, have to correct and rebuke those we disciple and lead, but always with love and patience. Proper rebuke can be life-changing and life-saving. We have to believe this or we will not do it.

Paul Fought Off Wolves

When wolves attacked Christ's flock, Paul became an unyielding lion. He was prepared to fight and to die for the church and the purity of the gospel message. (For evidence of this, see the book of Galatians.) Wherever he preached the gospel and planted churches, false teachers soon appeared to contradict the message of the cross.

Like Jesus Christ, Paul doesn't sound very loving or tolerant of these false teachers. Of anyone who preaches "a different gospel," he says, "let him be accursed" (Gal. 1:10). He calls false teachers deceivers, hypocrites, destroyers, evil workers, and dogs. And that they are. They masquerade as teachers of Christ when in reality they are agents of Satan:

> For such men are false apostles, deceitful workmen, disguising themselves as apostles of Christ. And no wonder, for even Satan disguises himself as an angel of light. So it is no surprise if his servants, also, disguise themselves as servants of righteousness. (2 Cor. 11:13-15)

Paul's solemn warnings are God's solemn warnings. Paul's intolerance of false teachers represents God's intolerance of false teachers. Paul's cries are those of a caring, loving father protecting his children from deception. His is a godly jealousy to preserve the purity of his beloved converts in the faith:

> I feel a divine jealousy for you, for I betrothed you to one husband, to present you as a pure virgin to Christ. But I am afraid that as the serpent deceived Eve by his cunning, your thoughts will be led astray from a sincere and pure devotion to Christ. (2 Cor. 11:2-3)

Using the Old Testament picture of a watchman on the wall of a city who was held responsible for the blood of those who died if he failed to warn the people of foreign invaders, Paul says, "I testify to you this day that I am innocent of the blood of all of you, for I did not shrink from declaring to you the whole counsel of God" (Acts 20:26-27).

John, James, Peter, Jude, and the writer of Hebrews also give strong warnings about the danger of being deceived by a false gospel or believing in a false Christ.

Paul Warned and Rebuked Fellow Believers

Not only did Paul warn of false teachers, he also protected the churches from internal strife and from returning to sexually immoral pagan behavior. Thus his letters are full of exhortations and admonitions.

With the Corinthians, Paul sometimes uses stern language. The reason for this language is that they were acting more like worldly-wise pagans than obedient followers of Jesus Christ. "These stern rebukes or severe warnings, however, were not inconsistent with his love. They stemmed from his love."[4]

All spiritual leaders have a solemn duty to admonish those they lead (1 Thess. 5:12). Paul tells Titus to "exhort and rebuke with all authority" (Titus 2:15), and at times, "rebuke ... sharply" (Titus 1:13). Paul charges Timothy to "preach the word ... reprove, rebuke, and exhort, with complete patience and teaching" (2 Tim. 4:2).

Sometimes shepherds in the church have to rebuke not the sheep but fellow leaders and teachers. Of sinning elders, Paul charges Timothy and the church to "rebuke them in the presence of all, so that the rest may stand in fear" (1 Tim. 5:20). On one occasion with the church at Antioch, Paul sharply rebuked Peter and his own colleague Barnabas for compromising the gospel and jeopardizing the unity of the

Sometimes shepherds in the church have to rebuke fellow leaders and teachers.

church. Peter, Barnabas, and other Jewish believers had stopped eating with their Gentile brothers and sisters in order to appease Jewish believers from Jerusalem (Gal. 2:11-14). Anticipating the disastrous effect of Peter's hypocrisy if left unchallenged for any length of time, Paul publicly confronted his brother in Christ. Paul understood that it was not the time for patient endurance but for taking immediate action and a strong, uncompromising stand.

Warning of danger, correcting wayward behavior, and rebuking sin are all part of leading with love. As Anthony Thiselton puts it, "The opposite of love is not correction but indifference."[5] As Christian leaders we will be required to admonish and rebuke. In fact, a good deal of time may be spent doing this work. It is an important aspect of ministry not to be neglected because it is used by God to rescue people from sin and deception. You will never know until heaven the full

"The opposite of love is not correction but indifference."

—Anthony Thiselton

extent of the good you have done for others by rebuking them about sin or warning them about false doctrine.

When I was in my early twenties, while helping lead a teen youth outreach, I tried to confront one of the Christian young men about his drug use. When I had no success, I went to his parents. This led to a year of bitter fighting and false accusations against me that resulted in my being dismissed as one of the youth leaders. The parents, influential in the church community, had believed their son's excuses and lies. It was a painful experience. A year later, the young man came to repentance over his drug use and confessed to his parents the lies he had told against me and others who had tried to help. He then apologized to all whom he had hurt. Later, he thanked me for caring enough to confront him about his drug addiction. Since that time, we have had a good relationship, and I have been a counselor and friend to him.

We all naturally want to avoid unpleasant encounters, but such confrontations, though tough, can literally save the life of those we love. "Those whom I love, I reprove," said the Lord Jesus (Rev. 3:19).

How to Warn and Rebuke with Love

When rebuking someone is necessary, it must be done with love and wisdom in the power of the Holy Spirit. Scripture tells us that Paul, though prepared to use a "rod" of discipline, would prefer dealing with his converts "with love in a spirit of gentleness" (1 Cor. 4:21). He handles people with gentleness, humility, kindness, patience, and love (2 Cor. 6:3-13; 10:1) and he warns with "tears" (Acts 20:31). He does not lord his authority over others but works with them, helping them stand firm in their faith (2 Cor. 1:24).

Paul's letters demonstrate masterful diplomacy and tact. He is severe and threatening only when there is no other option. Yet even then he cannot stop himself from alternately pouring out his heart in the most tender, endearing statements found anywhere in the New Testament.

The way in which we as leaders warn and correct others is crucial. Sinners reproving sinners is always a precarious work that must be done with love (1 Cor. 16:14). Admonishing, correcting, and reproving without love will only hurt people. But when given in love, a rebuke can be more readily received and a person's life can be

> **Sinners reproving sinners is always a precarious work that must be done with love.**

changed for the good. So consider these basic principles in confronting and rebuking with love.

Check Your Attitudes—Especially Anger

A well-known leader of a worldwide discipleship organization was asked what his main job was as head of such an organization. He responded, "Checking attitudes." Although he meant checking the attitudes of all within the organization, we can learn from his words. Before confronting anyone else, we must start by checking our own attitude. This makes all the difference between constructive and destructive confrontation and rebuke.

Guard your attitude against pride, vindictiveness, and impatience, but especially guard against anger. Don't rebuke or correct when you are angry. Wait until your anger is under the control of the Holy Spirit (Gal. 5:15-23). William Arnot offers excellent counsel in this matter:

> A wise man may indeed experience the heat [of anger], but he will do nothing till he cools again. When your clothes outside are on fire you wrap yourself in a blanket, if you can, and so smother the flame: in like manner, when your heart within has caught the fire of anger, your first business is to get the flame extinguished. Thereafter you will be in a better position to form a righteous judgment, and follow a safe course.[6]

Love, remember, is not easily provoked to anger (1 Cor. 13:5). But when you are angry, recognize that uncontrolled anger inflames emotions, exaggerates issues, and hinders godly correction. It tends to be less rational and more self-justifying. It deals with people harshly. Loud, threatening talk can echo in a person's mind for a lifetime. Thus the Bible says "be … slow to anger; for the anger of man does not produce the righteousness that God requires" (James 1:19-20). It also says, "A man of wrath stirs up strife, and one given to anger causes much transgression" (Prov. 29:22).

A calm and self-controlled spirit is essential to effective confrontation, as these verses point out:

* There is one whose rash words are like sword thrusts, but the tongue of the wise brings healing. (Prov. 12:18)
* Whoever restrains his words has knowledge, and he who has a cool spirit is a man of understanding. (Prov. 17:27)
* A hot-tempered man stirs up strife, but he who is slow to anger quiets contention. (Prov. 15:18)
* Whoever is slow to anger has great understanding, but he who has a hasty temper exalts folly. (Prov. 14:29)

When you have to rebuke a fellow believer, speaking with a gentle, calm voice eases tensions and makes the rebuke easier to receive:

* A soft answer turns away wrath, but a harsh word stirs up anger. (Prov. 15:1)
* A gentle tongue is a tree of life. (Prov. 15:4)
* With patience a ruler may be persuaded, and a soft tongue will break a bone. (Prov. 25:15)
* Let your speech always be gracious, seasoned with salt, so that you may know how you ought to answer each person. (Col. 4:6)

If you want to be a skillful confronter, always check your own attitude first and make sure you are under the control of the Holy Spirit. Be calm and self-controlled, and speak in a gracious, gentle way.

Resist Making Quick Accusations

No one likes to be falsely accused, so don't begin any confrontation with an accusation. Your accusation may be unjust, you may not have all the facts straight, you may be wrong. Begin by stating the problem objectively and asking the person for a response. An accusation is appropriate only after careful investigation and solid evidence has been established. When confronting, and especially when making accusations, follow the Golden Rule: "Whatever you wish that others would do to you, do also to them" (Matt. 7:12). You don't want to be unfairly accused, so don't accuse others.

Be a careful listener, ask lots of questions, be courteous, don't do all the talking, and let people know you will work hard to be fair and listen to their side of the story.

As an example, God gave us two eyes, two ears, and only one mouth. A lot of people never learn a lesson from that—which is that you ought always to use your eyes and ears twice as much as you use your mouth. Another way of putting it in electronic terms ... is that the purpose of the eyes and ears is to program the mouth. The problem with a lot of human relationships is that there is too much unprogrammed talk.[7]

Or, in the words of Scripture,

* Let every person be quick to hear, slow to speak, slow to anger. (James 1:19)
* If one gives an answer before he hears, it is his folly and shame.... The one who states his case first seems right, until the other comes and examines him. (Prov. 18:13, 17)

It was reported to a pastor that the church's youth leader was drinking alcohol at a restaurant while eating with the young people at an official church function. Parents heard this story and demanded that the youth leader be removed immediately from his position or they would leave the church. The pastor called an emergency elders' meeting. One elder said that the young man should be disciplined, another demanded that a letter be written dismissing him immediately before everyone in the church left, another surmised that he was an alcoholic. Finally, someone had the brilliant idea that they should talk to the youth leader and see what he had to say.

When they did so it became clear that it was a case of mistaken identity, but how quick people are to accuse. How easy it is to try, condemn, and execute someone without proper cause.

Think and Plan

Think before you act. Think of the words you will use before you reprove someone. Gracious words impart a blessing (Eph. 4:29) but harsh words do harm. The Bible says right words heal and wrong words cut like a knife.

- There is one whose rash words are like sword thrusts [that wound and kill], but the tongue of the wise brings healing. (Prov. 12:18)
- Gracious words are like a honeycomb, sweetness to the soul and health to the body. (Prov. 16:24)
- Death and life are in the power of the tongue. (Prov. 18:21)
- Let your speech always be gracious, seasoned with salt, so that you may know how you ought to answer each person. (Col. 4:6)

Furthermore, choose wisely the right place and time for reproof so that a person is not embarrassed in front of other people. "Love does no wrong to a neighbor" (Rom. 13:10). When reproving, don't unnecessarily offend or embarrass a person. Don't be like the man who angrily and loudly tore into the preacher at the front door of the church as everyone was leaving. He embarrassed and shocked everyone around. Of course, there are appropriate times for public rebuke, but that especially must be thought through carefully (1 Tim. 5:20; Gal. 2:14).

Use Patience and Scripture

The Bible states that reproof, rebuke, and exhortation are to be done "with complete patience and teaching" (2 Tim. 4:2). Dealing with stubborn doctrinal error or sinful behavior is always difficult work, so it demands "complete patience." Love is patient.

In addition, according to 2 Timothy 4:2, reproof is to be done with the use of Scripture. A few verses before, Paul says all Scripture is "breathed out by God" and is useful "for reproof, for correction" (2 Tim. 3:16). Therefore everything we need for warning and correcting others is provided by God in his Word. The New Testament writers used the Old Testament Scriptures to back up their warnings and teachings, and we should do the same.

Remember that Scripture will equip you for the task of correcting just as it equips you for "every good work" (2 Tim. 3:17). The more you know

Scripture, the more able you will be to effectively warn and reprove erring members in love.

I know a man, for example, who works with alcoholics. He admonishes them by carefully studying with them all that the Bible says about drunkenness, along with the biological facts about drunkenness. He helps them see God's perspective and the seriousness and destructiveness of drunkenness. His correction is not just his opinion; it is what God says. The Scriptures give weight to his words. This approach takes the focus off the reprover and places it on God and Scripture. This same approach can be used in dealing with other vices and addictions.

Be Gentle

During the Vietnam War, many mistakes were made, but some good lessons were learned as well. One such lesson was the wisdom of winning the hearts and minds of the Viet Cong and the North Vietnamese army regulars by promising that if they surrendered they would be treated with fairness, kindness, and generosity. They were promised nutritious food, medical treatment, education, good jobs, and an opportunity

> "The Lord's servant must not be quarrelsome but kind ... correcting his opponents with gentleness. God may perhaps grant them repentance leading to a knowledge of the truth, and they may escape from the snare of the devil."
>
> **2 Tim. 2:24-26**

to reunite with their families. The program was called Chieu Hoi (CHEW HOY, loosely translated: "open arms"). It was intended to encourage the enemy to give up the fight, but also to transform their thinking about communism. While the program didn't win the fanatical communist insurgents, it did help transform some 200,000 fighters. The communists took the success of this program of "open arms" seriously and did everything possible to destroy it. They feared the power of kindness and generosity, because it is ultimately more powerful than bombs and bullets.

The New Testament emphasizes treating people with gentleness, especially when correcting error or restoring a fallen believer. To be gentle with people is to be kind, tender, gracious, and calm—not harsh or combative. When confronting serious problems, Paul warns and corrects the Corinthians "by the meekness and gentleness of Christ" (2 Cor. 10:1). He enjoins believers to "restore" a fallen believer "in a spirit of gentleness" (Gal. 6:1). He tells Timothy that the "Lord's servant" must correct "his opponents with gentleness" (2 Tim. 2:24-25). The reason for treating opponents with gentleness is that it enhances the possibility of restoration: "God may per-

> **If you are not a positive encourager, you will probably be a poor admonisher.**

haps grant them repentance leading to a knowledge of the truth, and they may escape from the snare of the devil, after being captured by him to do his will" (2 Tim. 2:25-26). As a "man of God," Timothy is to pursue "gentleness" of character (1 Tim. 6:11), which will serve him well when dealing with different types of people and problems.

Correcting people with gentleness makes people more willing to listen and more open to a real change of heart and mind. In cultures where confrontation and rebuke are generally avoided, it is all the more necessary to be gracious and gentle when confronting sinful behavior.

Balance Reproof and Encouragement

Seek to balance out reproof with words of encouragement and hope. This is exactly what Paul does in his letters. To reproof, he adds encouragement, comfort, affirmation, and praise. Commentator Paul Barnett's remarks regarding Paul's ministry of encouragement bear repeating: "This pastoral skill, expressed in encouragement—even when there were other matters to redress—is a quality of ministry worth pondering."[8]

After the stormy discipline and restoration of a rebellious member, Paul assures the church in Corinth that all along he was confident they would do the right thing:

> I am acting with great boldness toward you; I have great pride in you;
> I am filled with comfort. In all our affliction, I am overflowing with joy.
> … I rejoice, because I have perfect confidence in you. (2 Cor. 7:4, 16)

When my brother-in-law's father died unexpectedly, I called him to express my sorrow and see how he was doing. Speaking of his father, with whom he was very close, he said, "I will really miss him. My father was a great encourager." What a wonderful commendation from a son! A son would be eager to take correction from such a father. In fact, most people would respond better to a rebuke from a person who has already been encouraging them on the path of life. So when you must deal with the bad, remember also to look for the good in people and point out anything that is commendable or worthy of praise (Phil. 4:8). If you are not a positive encourager, you will probably be a poor admonisher.

Pray

Pray for wisdom, courage, and self-control. Also pray that the Lord would prepare the other person or persons to receive your reproof. *When people do not want to receive correction, they will invariably accuse you of not acting in love toward them.* They will try to turn the table and make you the issue. So be sure in your own mind that you have done your best to act in love. If you have, then they are the ones who are not responding in love.

In the words of wise King Solomon, proud scoffers do not accept correction but hate those who reprove. The wise, on the other hand, delight in correction and love those who reprove and instruct them:

> Whoever corrects a scoffer gets himself abuse,
>   and he who reproves a wicked man incurs injury.
> Do not reprove a scoffer, or he will hate you;
>   reprove a wise man, and he will love you.
> Give instruction to a wise man, and he will be still wiser;
>   teach a righteous man, and he will increase in learning. (Prov. 9:7-9)

Notes to Chapter 15

1. Ezek. 3:17-21; 33:7-8.
2. Matt. 16:8, 11; Mark 8:17-18, 32-33; 16:14; Luke 9:41; 12:29.
3. A. B. Bruce, *The Training of the Twelve*, 2d ed. (1877; reprint ed., Grand Rapids, Mich.: Kregel, 1988), 14.
4. Roy B. Zuck, *Teaching as Paul Taught* (Grand Rapids, Mich.: Baker, 1998), 104.
5. Anthony C. Thiselton, *The First Epistle to the Corinthians,* NIGTC (Grand Rapids, Mich.: Eerdmans, 2000), 1089.
6. William Arnot, *Studies in Proverbs* (1884; reprint ed., Grand Rapids, Mich.: Kregel, 1978), 398.

7. Reuel L. Howe, "The Responsibility of the Preaching Task," *Preaching: A Journal of Homiletics* 4 (November-December 1969): 10.

8. Paul Barnett, *The Second Epistle to the Corinthians*, NICNT (Grand Rapids, Mich.: Eerdmans, 1997), 364.

Chapter 16

Disciplining and Restoring the Wayward

*The Lord disciplines the one he loves, and chastises
every son whom he receives.*
Heb. 12:6

A man in the church was openly cohabiting with his father's wife, his step-mother. He was living in an incestuous relationship, and everyone in the church knew about it. What was worse, except for a few people, the church was complacent about the whole matter.

This kind of illicit sexual relationship was not tolerated by Roman society or Jewish.[1] Instead of grieving over sin, the church was arrogant. It tolerated grievous sin, although it was "God's temple" (1 Cor. 3:16) and the "body of Christ" (1 Cor. 12:27). You can read about this true story in 1 Corinthians 5.

Paul, the founding missionary of the church, was not a passive leader. Instead of waiting to see what would happen, he called for immediate action and directed the congregation to expel the man from the congregation:

- Let him who has done this be removed from among you. (1 Cor. 5:2)
- Deliver this man to Satan for the destruction of the flesh, so that his spirit may be saved in the day of the Lord. (1 Cor. 5:5)
- Cleanse out the old leaven. (1 Cor. 5:7)
- I am writing to you not to associate with … not even to eat with such a one. (1 Cor. 5:11)
- Purge the evil person from among you. (1 Cor. 5:13)

151

A Seeming Contradiction

The question that troubles many people today is how can Paul demand such severe public discipline yet in the same letter write some of the most glowing words ever written about love (1 Cor. 13). Doesn't Paul say, "Let all that you do be done in love" (1 Cor. 16:14)? Doesn't he say that love is "patient," that love "endures all things" (1 Cor. 13:4, 7)? The answer to this seeming contradiction is that love can be both tender and stern.

Christian love demands action—even painful action—to save a sinning member and an entire church. The Bible says, "For the Lord disciplines the one he loves, and chastises every son whom he receives" (Heb. 12:6). Speaking to the lukewarm church at Laodicea, Jesus warns, "Those whom I love, I reprove and discipline"(Rev. 3:19). The Lord loves his people, so he disciplines them, he chastens them—and at times severely.

> **Christian love demands action, even painful action, to save sinning members or an entire church.**

Love is not just happy smiles or pleasant words. A critical test of genuine love is whether we are willing to confront and discipline those we care for. Nothing is more difficult than disciplining a brother or sister in Christ who is trapped in sin. It is always agonizing work—messy, complicated, often unsuccessful, emotionally exhausting, and potentially divisive. This is why most church leaders avoid discipline at all costs. But that is not love. It is lack of courage and disobedience to the Lord Jesus Christ, who himself laid down instructions for the discipline of an unrepentant believer:

> If he refuses to listen to them, tell it to the church. And if he refuses to listen even to the church, let him be to you as a Gentile and a tax collector. Truly, I say to you, whatever you bind on earth shall be bound in heaven, and whatever you loose on earth shall be loosed in heaven. (Matt. 18:17-18)

Love Acts in Discipline

Significantly, the apostle who made the greatest statements about love and wrote the most about it also wrote the most about church discipline.

* The church at Ephesus was in the death grip of false teachers. To save the church, Paul disciplined two of the ringleaders, Hymenaeus and Alexander. Regarding the discipline of these two men, Paul writes to Timothy, "I have handed [them] over to Satan that they may learn not to blaspheme" (1 Tim. 1:20).

* Paul instructs Titus and the churches on the island of Crete: "As for a person who stirs up division, after warning him once and then twice, have nothing more to do with him" (Titus 3:10).

* To the Christians in Rome, Paul similarly says, "watch out for those who cause divisions and create obstacles contrary to the doctrine that you have been taught; avoid them" (Rom. 16:17).

* In the letter of 1 Corinthians, Paul reminds the Corinthians that he had previously written them not to associate with an unrepentant, immoral Christian. But they had misunderstood him. So again, he writes: "But now I am writing to you not to associate with anyone who bears the name of brother if he is guilty of sexual immorality ... not even to eat with such a one" (1 Cor. 5:11).

* Some believers in the church at Thessalonica were lazy; they were idle. They did not work to provide for their own needs but sponged off others. Paul commands the church to discipline these people. The future of the church and its witness on the unbelieving community hinged on this practical issue: "Now we command ... that you keep away from any brother who is walking in idleness.... If anyone does not obey what we say in this letter, take note of that person and have nothing to do with him, that he may be ashamed. Do not regard him as an enemy, but warn him as a brother" (2 Thess. 3:6, 14-15).

* In 2 Corinthians, Paul repeatedly expresses his intense love for the believers. Yet because of their sinful behavior he also threatens discipline, "being ready to punish every disobedience" (2 Cor. 10:6). "I warned those who sinned before and all the others, and I warn them now while absent, as I did when present on my second visit, that if I come again I will not spare them" (2 Cor. 13:2). But the prospect of having to disci-

pline members of the church grieved him. Paul wanted them to judge and correct themselves. So he warns them to repent and correct their ways before he comes to visit them again: "For this reason I write these things while I am away from you, that when I come I may not have to be severe [in discipline]" (2 Cor. 13:10).

If Paul did not love the Corinthians, he would walk away from them and let them flounder in their own cesspool of sin. Instead, he is proactive. He confronts, warns, writes, visits, and even humbles himself before them (2 Cor. 2:5-10; 12:21). Such are the works of "genuine love" in Christian ministry (2 Cor. 6:6).

Love Acts to Restore

Genuine love not only disciplines, it heals and restores. The key New Testament example of successful church discipline and loving restoration appears in the letter of 2 Corinthians, which gives us a special glimpse into the loving heart of one of God's greatest servants. The sorrow, anguish, and tears Paul personally experienced as a result of the church's sin and disobedience is part of the price a loving leader pays in the work of discipline and restoration. Here is the story.

After writing the letter of 1 Corinthians, further news reached Paul of the deteriorating situation in that troubled church. Paul responded by making a quick, pastoral visit to Corinth from the city of Ephesus where he was living. But the visit proved to be a disaster. Scholars call this visit the "Painful Visit."[2]

When he arrived at Corinth, an unnamed individual withstood Paul's admonitions, insulting and humiliating him.[3] But worse, the congregation was reluctant to side with Paul and to discipline "the offender." This caused a terrible strain in the relationship between Paul and the Corinthians. Something had to be done.

Writing a Severe Letter

After returning to the city of Ephesus, Paul wrote a stern letter to the church urging it to take action against the offender and to judge its own sinful behavior. This letter has been lost to us; it is not in the New Testament.

Bible scholars call it the "Severe Letter," or sometimes the "Tearful Letter" or the "Sorrowful Letter."[4]

In the letter of 2 Corinthians, Paul reveals that one of the reasons for writing the Severe Letter, was to let the Corinthians "know the love" that he had for them:

> For I wrote to you out of much affliction and anguish of heart [in the Severe Letter] and with many tears, not to cause you pain but to let you know *the abundant love that I have for you.* (2 Cor. 2:4; italics added)

Paul did not write the Severe Letter to strike back at them in revenge for the pain they had caused him, but to show the depth of his love for them. Love, not impatient anger, compelled him to confront the church's moral laxity. By confronting them and writing to them, he was actually proving his love for them. His "tears" were the tears of a loving parent having to act

Paul "urges forgiveness and reconciliation with equal vigor" as he previously called for corrective discipline.

sternly with loved ones, even causing them pain. Discipline and rebuke were no easier for Paul than they are for us.

Although the letter was severe, it worked. In response to the Severe Letter, the church, for the most part, repented and took formal disciplinary action against the offender.[5]

As a result of that discipline, the man repented. Now a new issue arose. What does the church do with him? Again, Paul knows exactly what to do: The church needs to forgive and restore him to loving fellowship. Paul "urges forgiveness and reconciliation with equal vigor" as he previously called for corrective discipline.[6]

Affirming Love

Love heals the sorrowing soul unlike any other medicine. Here is a living example of 1 Corinthians 13 in action. Paul calls on the church to "forgive and comfort" the repentant member (2 Cor. 2:7). Restoration of the penitent sinner is just as vital to the local church as the discipline itself.

Phillip Hughes aptly comments:

> it is no less a scandal to cut off the penitent sinner from all hope of re-entry into the comfort and security of the fellowship of the redeemed community than it is to permit flagrant wickedness to continue un-punished in the Body of Christ.[7]

Not only was there need for forgiveness and comfort, but there was need for love. Compassionately Paul writes, "I beg you to reaffirm your love for him" (2 Cor. 2:8). He doesn't want the restored member to have to wonder about the church's love. He urges the church to make perfectly clear its love, probably by means of a formal public statement.[8] Like the rejoicing father running out to greet the prodigal son with open arms and joy (Luke 15:11-32), the church needed to welcome its sorrowful son with forgiveness, comfort, and love.

> **"I beg you to reaffirm your love for him."**
> **2 Cor. 2:8**

Love's Connection with Discipline and Restoration

Paul's dealings with the Corinthians demonstrate that corrective church discipline and restoration are inseparable from love. This is true in a number of ways.

First, love for the Lord Jesus Christ compels us to take corrective disciplinary action. Church discipline is Christ's command (Matt. 18:15-20), and love obeys his commands: "If you love me, you will keep my commandments" (John 14:15). So the exercise of church discipline demonstrates love for Christ.

Second, love feels moral indignation at evil and its senseless destruction of loved ones. Love abhors what is evil and holds fast to what is good (Rom. 12:9). Love doesn't "call evil good and good evil" (Isa. 5:20). "O you who love the Lord," says the Psalmist, "hate evil!" (Ps. 97:10). Love never downplays the seriousness of sin and its corrupting powers, nor does it minimize standards of right or wrong. Thus loving leaders cannot be apathetic toward a sinning member. They must act to correct and rescue. Discipline is a mark of loving leadership.

Church discipline is not a shameful, medieval practice. Every responsible society has a code of discipline to protect itself from unlawful behavior among its members. This is true for the police, military, legal and medical societies, and for the political and corporate worlds.

Sin must always be dealt with (either personally or corporately) because it is its nature to destroy: "For the wages of sin is death" (Rom. 6:23). So for the good of the entire local church as well as the impenitent sinner, God requires corrective discipline. The truth is, as James Denny writes, "The judgment of the Church is the instrument of God's love, and the moment it is accepted in the sinful soul it begins to work as a redemptive force."⁹

Third, Christians are to love one another with a special brotherly and sisterly love. What kind of brotherly or sisterly love simply allows a family member to wander off in sin or error from the family? James, therefore, encourages believers to act to save a straying brother or sister. He concludes his letter by saying that if a brother or sister "wanders from the truth" and one "brings him [or her] back" to the truth, he has

Discipline is a mark of loving leadership.

done a good thing and saved the straying member's "soul from death and will cover a multitude of sins" (James 5:19-20). We are our "brother's keeper" (Gen. 4:9). Taking the initiative to discipline and restore is an unselfish act of brotherly love.

Fourth, love provides the right attitudes for exercising church discipline and restoration. Love acts patiently and kindly; love is compassionate; it feels for the misery of the impenitent sinner and seeks to relieve pain and rescue from death. Loving hands are healing hands, both tender and firm. (See chapters 15 and 17 for practical suggestions for dealing in love with difficult situations and people.) When, therefore, we help restore a fallen brother or sister through loving discipline, we are, in the words of Scripture, bearing "one another's burdens" and fulfilling "the law of Christ" (Gal. 6:2).

Love's Connection with Judging Others

In the Sermon on the Mount, Jesus says, "Judge not, that you be not judged" (Matt. 7:1). This verse has become a modern day mantra. People who have never read one word of the Gospels know this verse. It proves to them that

Jesus was a teacher of tolerance; he was nonjudgmental and nondogmatic; he would condemn no one; he would never judge anyone. Unfortunately, even some believers misuse this verse. They say we have no right to exercise church discipline, to judge another person, or to make an adverse opinion about a person's behavior or belief! But plainly this is a misuse of Jesus' words.

Jesus is not forbidding all judging, that would be absurd. To do so would be condemning himself because no one criticized the Pharisees and scribes more than Jesus Christ. Later in the same chapter, Jesus calls his disciples to judge whether a teacher is a genuine teacher of the truth or just a wolf in sheep's clothing (Matt. 7:15-20). We are not to naively shut our eyes to evil behavior or false doctrine; we are to be discerning. In John 7:24 Jesus tell us, "Do not judge by appearances, but judge with right judgment."

> "The judgment of the Church is the instrument of God's love, and the moment it is accepted in the sinful soul it begins to work as a redemptive force."
> —James Denny

What Jesus prohibits in Matthew 7:1-6 is sinful, improper judging. It is the hypocrisy of condemning others but failing to see one's own glaring sins. Jesus forbids self-righteous criticism, a hypercritical spirit, and a harsh, fault-finding mindset. In pride and self-righteousness, the Pharisees and scribes were in the habit of acting as if they themselves were God. They were unforgiving and unkind in their judgments, and they had not judged their own hearts of sin.

Jesus warns in verse 2 that how we judge others (assuming we will and must) will determine how we, in turn, will be judged by others, especially God: "For with the judgment you pronounce you will be judged, and with the measure you use it will be measured to you." Those who judge others without mercy will receive the same treatment. But those who judge with humility, kindness, and grace will receive the same.

In verse 3, Jesus asks the hypocritical Pharisees, "Why do you see the speck that is in your brother's eye, but do not notice the log that is in your own eye?" (Matt. 7:3). It's easy to see the small sins and faults in others but fail to see one's own sins which are far worse and more repugnant to God. Such judgment of others is hypocrisy! "You hypocrite, first take the log out of your own eye, and then you will see clearly to take the speck out of your brother's eye" (Matt. 7:5).

Rightful Judging of Others

There is nothing wrong with wanting to help remove specks of sin from a person's life. Love seeks the good of what is loved, and specks of dust in the eye hurt, so they need to be removed. But first, Jesus says, deal with logs of self-righteousness, pride, anger, and hypocrisy in your own life, then you will be able to see clearly to help others. What Jesus calls for is judgment of self and personal examination of your own sins. Only after examining yourself honestly will you be in a position to judge others with a clear eye: "then you will see clearly to take the speck out of your brother's eye" (Matt. 7:5). Proper judging must be done with a humble mind and a clean heart.

Jesus concludes: "Do not give dogs what is holy, and do not throw your pearls before pigs, lest they trample them underfoot and turn to attack you" (Matt. 7:6). After exhorting his disciples to avoid judging as the hypocrites do, Jesus warns them of the opposite danger—being undiscerning and naïve. We, as they, are not to be foolish toward people who utterly despise the great truths of the gospel. In some situations, it is even proper to refrain from giving the gospel message to such people, which is exactly what Jesus did with King Herod (Luke 23:9).[10]

This teaching is meant to protect the church and the gospel message from people who act like dogs and pigs in regard to the glorious truths of Christianity. Such people are antagonists who hate the truth and will seek only to destroy it and those who proclaim it! So Christians are called to be discerning, that is, able to make right assessments about people.

Making proper moral and spiritual judgments about doctrine and conduct is required by Scripture. The gospel would be lost to the world and the church would be assimilated into secular society if we did not make discriminating judgments between truth and error, Christ and Satan. Thus the Scripture commands, "do not believe every spirit, but test the spirits to see whether they are from God, for many false prophets have gone out into the world" (1 John 4:1). Jesus Christ wholeheartedly commends the church at Ephesus because it did not tolerate "those who are evil" and hated "the works of the Nicolaitans," which Jesus also hated (Rev. 2:2, 6). Love abhors lies and falsehood because of its destructive consequences to people.

> **Christ requires the local church to judge immoral behavior among its members so it will not be assimilated into an immoral world.**

Christ also requires the local church to judge immoral behavior among its members so it will not be assimilated into an immoral world. This was one of the problems in the church at Corinth: It didn't judge unrepentant sin in its midst (1 Cor. 5:12).

Judging fellow believers' sinful behavior or judging false doctrine, therefore, is commanded by Christ and his apostles. It is not to be done with self-righteous condemnation but with humility of mind, gentleness of spirit, and fear of the Lord. As Jesus says, "Judge with right judgment" (John 7: 24). And be mindful of Paul's warning, "Keep watch on yourself, lest you too be tempted" (Gal. 6:1).

Love's Connection to Tolerance

Paul's instruction to the Christians at Corinth to judge and expel one of their members for sexual sin seems to contemporary, secular-minded people to be insensitive to the couple's physical and emotional needs, judgmental of another's lifestyle, divisive, unloving, and intolerant. Such a response is understandable given the fact that secular-minded people reject God's moral absolutes as revealed in Scripture. They are committed to the philosophy of moral relativism that views all religious claims as equally valid and all truth claims and values as culturally created. They redefine *tolerance* to mean not only respect and forbearance with regard to disagreement, but approval and acceptance of others' moral and religious beliefs.

> "Obviously the modern idea of toleration has turned upon itself, producing in many cases greater bigotry than anything it sought to eradicate."
>
> —A. J. Conyers

Paul's call for discipline is, therefore, viewed by some as mean-spirited and intolerant. Unfortunately, even some Christians who profess to believe the truths of the gospel and accept the divine authority of Scripture think along the same lines. They are unwilling to accept the idea of church discipline or to follow scriptural principles in this regard. For Christians who live in an ocean of secularism and relativism that despises God and deplores the Scripture, the only hope for understanding genuine tolerance and love as God defines these terms is through renewing the mind by saturating it with the Word of God (Rom. 12:2; John 17:17).

So what is God's definition of *tolerance*? What does his Word have to say on this subject?

Love's Tolerance

Genuine Christian love is tolerant in the sense that it is forbearing and kind toward those with whom there is disagreement. Paul reminds believers of the importance of "bearing with [or showing tolerance for] one another in love" (Eph. 4:2). Without the virtue of tolerance rightly understood, it would be impossible to live together in marriage, church, family, or society.

Christian love is also tolerant in that it is humble-minded and modest about itself and its knowledge. It is not arrogant or self-superior. It is not easily angered by disagreement. It forgives and doesn't hold grudges. Moreover, Christian love calls us to do good to our enemies, even to those who call us intolerant because we believe Jesus Christ to be the one and true Savior of the world. Christian love does not allow for mocking or coercing those with whom we disagree. Instead, love says, "whatever you wish that others would do to you, do also to them" (Matt. 7:12).

In witnessing of Christ to those who reject what we believe or are hostile to our beliefs, the Scripture says, "Let your speech [with the unbeliever] always be gracious, seasoned with salt" and be "prepared to make a defense to anyone who asks you for a reason for the hope that is in you; yet do it with gentleness and respect" (Col. 4:6; 1 Peter 3:15-16). Christians are not permitted to hate those who disagree with us. We love them and pray for them. We seek to persuade them of the truth of the gospel with reason, gentleness, and compassion.

Christians are taught that all people are created in God's image and are valuable in God's eyes, so all people are to be treated with respect and love. As the Scripture says, "Let your reasonableness [or 'gentle forbearance'] be known to everyone [to unbelievers especially]" (Phil. 4:5).

Love's Intolerance

There is also a legitimate sense in which Christian love is intolerant. It is not tolerant in the sense of approving or accepting that which is immoral or false as defined by God's Word. Love cannot be tolerant of that which destroys people's lives or spreads lies about the gospel. "Love is the fulfilling of the law," not the breaking of God's law (Rom. 13:10). Love "does not rejoice at wrongdoing, but rejoices with the truth" (1 Cor. 13:6).

The fact is, no one is tolerant of everything. *Tolerance* itself is a neutral word. It is what one is tolerant of that makes it good or bad. Even those who cry the loudest for tolerance claim to have "zero tolerance" for sexual child abuse, rape, and racial discrimination—and so they should. Despite their assertion that they are moral relativists, they do have moral absolutes, and they are prepared to fight for them. They are more than willing to take strong disciplinary action in the workplace and in government agencies against those who violate those moral absolutes.

Ironically, the so-called tolerance of secular relativism is quite intolerant of those who disagree with its philosophy of truth and ideological commitments. Numerous books and articles, from both secular and religious perspectives, have exposed the arrogance and hypocrisy of the relativist's tolerance.[11] A. J. Conyers writes, "Obviously the modern idea of toleration has turned upon itself, producing in many cases greater bigotry than anything it sought to eradicate."[12]

In fact, the word *tolerance* is being used as a club to intimidate and marginalize people who don't fall to their knees before the god of moral and religious relativism. The word itself is actually used to foster intolerance of all dissenters of secular relativism and its religious counterparts. In one country famous for its boast of tolerance, a prominent sign reads, "Death to the Intolerant." C. S. Lewis complained that it was from the so-called undogmatic and tolerant that he experienced the most intolerant, bitter treatment.[13] This new tolerance sees the specks of intolerance in the eyes of others, but can't see its own logs of intolerance, dogmatism, pride, absolutism, discrimination, authoritarianism, and lack of love.

In contrast, the Bible-believing, evangelical community believes that God has given universal, objective moral standards and that he is the ultimate authority to which all people will someday answer. His moral standards are to be maintained among his people. Thus when a professing believer continually violates God's moral standard and refuses to respond to loving appeals for repentance, God requires loving corrective discipline.

It is not intolerant to discipline immoral sexual behavior. It is not intolerant to expose lies or criticize false teaching. It is not intolerant to hold moral convictions or to believe one knows truth. The world does the same. The most secular-minded people hold tightly to certain moral convictions.

Ultimately, then, refusal to confront a fellow believer's sin or false teaching in the name of tolerance and love is counterfeit tolerance and distorted love.

Paul loved the believers at Corinth, so he acted decisively in discipline. He was not mean-spirited or intolerant. The situation called for immediate corrective action to save the church from moral and spiritual corruption (1 Cor. 5:6-8). Tolerance is not always the appropriate response. It is possible to be tolerant of the wrong things. It is possible to tolerate what God does not. Tolerance is not the supreme virtue. Indeed, a false, inflated view of tolerance will destroy a church or a nation.

> Refusal to confront a fellow believer's sin or false teaching in the name of tolerance and love is counterfeit tolerance and distorted love.

Paul disciplined the immoral man and called for the church to do the same because he loved the church. Paul could not tolerate the man's immoral behavior because of love for God, love for the truth, love for the church, and love for the sinning member. It was by the stern discipline imposed by Paul, not the church's lackadaisical tolerance, that the sinning member received genuine hope and help—that his "spirit may be saved in the day of the Lord" (1 Cor. 5:5).

Notes to Chapter 16

1. Lev. 18:8; 20:11; Deut. 22:30; 27:20.

2. 2 Cor. 2:1; 12:14, 21; 13:1-2.

3. 2 Cor. 2:5-10; 7:12.

4. Some Bible teachers believe the "Severe Letter" to be 1 Corinthians, but most scholars today believe it to be a lost letter written between the letters of 1 and 2 Corinthians.

5. 2 Cor. 2:5-10; 7:11-12, 15.

6. Paul Barnett, *The Second Epistle to the Corinthians*, NICNT (Grand Rapids, Mich.: Eerdmans, 1997), 127.

7. Philip Hughes, *Paul's Second Epistle to the Corinthians*, NICNT (Grand Rapids, Mich.: Eerdmans, 1962), 66-67.

8. The Greek verb for "reaffirm" *(kyrosai)* is a legal term meaning "confirm" or "ratify," which most likely indicates a formal reinstatement to fellowship after formal public discipline.

9. James Denny, *The Second Epistle to the Corinthians*, The Expositor's Bible (New York: Funk&Wagnalls, 1900), 75.

10. Matt. 10:14; 15:14; Acts 13:44-51; 18:5-6; 28:17-28.

11. For an easy-to-read book on the secular liberal idea of tolerance read: Josh McDowell and Bob Hostetler, *The New Tolerance* (Wheaton, Ill.: Tyndale, 1998). For a more in-depth analysis of the new tolerance, see Brad Stetson and Joseph G. Conti, *The Truth about Tolerance: Pluralism, Diversity, and the Culture Wars* (Downers Grove, Ill.: InterVarsity, 2005).

12. A. J. Conyers, quoted in Stetson and Conti, *The Truth about Tolerance*, 113.

13. Lyle W. Dorsett, *Seeking the Secret Place: The Spiritual Formation of C. S. Lewis* (Grand Rapids, Mich.: Brazos Press, 2004), 77.

Chapter 17

Managing Conflict
a 'More Excellent Way'

Love covers a multitude of sins.
1 Peter 4:8

The first sin recorded in Genesis after Adam's and Eve's disobedience is that of Cain killing his brother Abel. Humans have been killing each other ever since. One of the dreadful consequences of "sin" entering the world (Rom. 5:12) is human warfare, and our history can be traced through endless wars and divisions.

Unfortunately, the same is true of God's people. What's worse, our battles are not even always over major issues such as unorthodox versus orthodox doctrine or liberal versus conservative views. Bible-believing churches that enjoy 95 percent agreement on all fundamental doctrinal issues will fight and divide over the most petty differences. Jewish philosopher Benedict de Spinoza made this distressing observation about Christians and the way they quarrel:

> I have often wondered, that persons who make boast of professing the Christian religion, namely, love, joy, peace, temperance, and charity to all men, should quarrel with such rancorous animosity, and display daily towards one another such bitter hatred, that this, rather than the virtues which they claim, is the readiest criteria of their faith.[1]

One of Satan's most successful strategies for keeping churches weak and ineffective is infighting and unresolved conflicts. *This is a life-and-death issue in our local churches.* So as a Christian leader, you will not only have

165

to face many conflicts, you will have to manage them according to biblical principles.

How Love Handles Conflict

There is nothing wrong with Christians disagreeing with one another or trying to persuade another of the rightness of a particular position. What is wrong, however, is loveless conflict that ends in hate and bitterness. "But if you bite and devour one another, watch out that you are not consumed by one another" (Gal. 5:15). *You as a leader need to be able to teach the principles of Christian love that help reduce, temper, and heal conflict.* But before you can teach those principles to others, you must first know them and model them in your own life.

In his book *The Mark of the Christian*, Francis Schaeffer, speaking from years of experience, says it is important to recognize the significance of not just the disagreement at hand but the words, actions, and attitudes displayed in the midst of the conflict:

> I have observed one thing *among true Christians* in their differences in many countries: What divides and severs true Christian groups and Christians—what leaves a bitterness that can last for 20, 30, 40 years (or for 50 or 60 years in a son's or daughter's memory)—is not the issue of doctrine or belief that caused the differences in the first place. Invariably, it is a lack of love—and the bitter things that are said by true Christians in the midst of differences.[2]

Love promotes the virtues that unite (patience, kindness, humility, forgiveness) and prohibits the many vices that divide and accentuate disagreement (jealousy, arrogance, selfishness, unforgiveness). No wonder Paul points to the "more excellent way" of love as a solution to the conflicts among the Christians at Corinth. The fifteen descriptions that explain the way of love should be read in the light of church conflict (1 Cor. 13:4-7).

Love Acts under the Control of the Holy Spirit

When facing conflict, the first and most important thing to remember is this: Be Spirit-controlled, not out of control.[3] Do not allow yourself to be controlled by the flesh and the devil. The flesh produces nothing but strife, anger, and division: "Now the works of the flesh are evident ... enmity, strife, jealousy, fits of anger, rivalries, dissensions, divisions, envy" (Gal. 5:19-21). If, however, you are controlled by the Holy Spirit, you will act in love and with self-control. You will be kind, gentle, patient, and peaceful (Gal. 5:22-23). A Spirit-controlled leader handles conflict according to the "more excellent way."

Love Curbs the Destructive Power of Anger

In any conflict, beware of anger (Eph. 4:26-27). Uncontrolled anger kills love and divides people. Beware especially of angry words, which only in-flame passions and distort the issues being debated. When people become angry, they often don't care what they say or do. They throw un-loving words around like daggers that wound and kill; they use

When facing conflict, be Spirit-controlled, not out of control.

them to get revenge. Such words hurt deeply and can stick in someone's mind for a lifetime.

Church leaders need to remember that as ones who are supposed to be examples of God's love, they are in the construction business, not the de-struction business. Psalm 145:8 says, "The Lord is gracious and merciful, slow to anger and abounding in steadfast love." Loving leaders reflect God's character to others and are not easily provoked to anger (1 Cor. 13:5). They are slow to anger and patient. Love should govern the way we talk and re-spond to people. When involved in sharp disagreement with a brother or sister, for example, we should choose our words carefully, soften the polem-ics, and control our emotions. Remember James 1:19: "be quick to hear, slow to speak, slow to anger." Unfortunately, when disputes arise, many Christians reinterpret this passage to mean "slow to hear, quick to speak, quick to become angry."

Love Acts with a Humble Spirit

Behind most church fights and unresolved divisions is ugly human pride. And the worst kind of pride is religious pride, the Pharisaical pride of self-righteousness and superiority.

The Bible says, "By insolence [pride] comes nothing but strife" (Prov. 13:10). Because of pride, Diotrephes, for example, liked to put himself first (3 John 9). He was selfish. Loving leaders are selfless. They are "not arrogant" (1 Cor. 13:4). They don't have an inflated opinion of themselves or an ego that stirs up strife.

When dealing with the Philippian church, Paul's solution is for each person to adopt Christ's attitude of humility (Phil. 2:5): "Have this mind among yourselves, which is yours in Christ Jesus." This attitude of humility is essential to tempering conflict, to resolving differences, to really hearing other people, to seeing our own faults, to submitting one to another, and to forgiving and reconciling. Peter puts it this way: "Clothe yourselves, all of you, with humility toward one another" (1 Peter 5:5).

Love should govern the way we talk and respond to people.

Imagine a large room full of pianos. If you were to tune all of them with one tuning fork, they all would be in perfect tune with each other. But if you were to tune the pianos one with another, they would soon be out of tune with each other. The same is true in the local church. Each believer is to tune his or her attitude to Christ's attitude, and that attitude is humility. There is a saying, "attitude is everything," but for the Christian, it must be taken one step further: "Christ's attitude is everything."

Love Pursues Peace

Peacemaking is an act of love blessed by the Lord Jesus Christ (Matt. 5:9). It is necessary for the unity and growth of the local church. To the struggling Christians in Rome, Paul writes, "Let love be genuine…. If possible, so far as it depends on you, live peaceably with all" (Rom. 12:9, 18). Later he adds, "let us pursue what makes for peace" (Rom. 14:19). And to encourage unity among Jew and Gentile believers, Paul writes, "Walk in a manner worthy of the calling to which you have been called, with all humility and patience, bearing with one another in love, eager to maintain the unity of the Spirit in the bond of peace" (Eph. 4:1-3). Church leaders, then, are to aggressively pursue peace and harmony in the church. They must be peacemakers, not fighters. That is why the qualifications for church elders require them to be "not violent but gentle" and "not quarrelsome" (1 Tim. 3:3).

Peacemaking is hard work. It takes a lot of wisdom and self-control. It means putting the good of others first. Denying themselves, peacemakers make every effort to guide those in conflict toward constructive solutions, justice, and Christian reconciliation (Phil 4:2-3). Sadly, they are often misunderstood and maligned as compromisers and people pleasers.

When we talk about peacemaking, however, we are not talking about peace at any price or surrendering truth under the guise of love. That is not true peace. Dennis Johnson warns of the risks of such so-called peace:

> God's peace does not peacefully coexist with falsehood, sham, or injustice; so God's peacemakers cannot simply ignore peace-destroying sin and error, any more than a surgeon can simply close up an infected wound: an abscess is bound to develop.[4]

We must remember that many church conflicts are not about the central truths of the gospel but are about secondary issues, personality clashes, program changes. These can and should be peacefully resolved by Spirit-filled, loving leaders. One such leader confronted his church, which was at war with itself. This pastor stood up and publicly declared: "It is time to 'wage peace.'" Waging peace is hard, self-sacrificing work, but it must be done.

Love Covers a Multitude of Sins

With his typical humor, Howard Hendricks remarks, "Many of us are like porcupines trying to huddle together on a bitter cold night to keep each other warm, but we continually poke and hurt each other the closer we get." At no time do we as brothers and sisters "poke and hurt each other" more painfully than during conflict. Without fervent love we could not survive such injuries and maintain family unity. That is why Peter writes, "Above all, keep loving one another earnestly, since love covers a multitude of sins" (1 Peter 4:8).

"Waging peace" is hard, self-sacrificing work....

Love covers all kinds of offenses, hurts, annoyances, disappointments, and sins that we all suffer because of others. Only love has the power to freely and repeatedly forgive, to truly seek to understand people's weaknesses and complexities, to put things into proper perspective, and to put a blanket over other people's faults. Jesus' love for his disciples covered their many sins. He understood their weaknesses, but his love covered them all; otherwise, he couldn't have lived with them.

This is in no way to imply that love ignores or condones sin. Love covers a multitude of sins, not all sins. At times, love requires exposure and discipline of sin for the welfare of an individual as well as the church. Love knows when to cover and when to expose for the purpose of redemption and restoration.

Paul's way of saying "love covers" is to say that love is not resentful (1 Cor. 13:5). Clinging to grievances and wounds keeps conflicts from being resolved. Love refuses to keep a record of injuries and offenses, but chooses to forgive. Forgiveness is one of the most important qualities of love (Eph. 4:32; Col. 3:13).

Loving leaders will not hold grudges or perpetuate warfare with those who have caused injury or offense. They demonstrate great understanding of people and their problems. They forgive and reconcile. They cover a multitude of sins.

Because love forgives, it brings healing. In the words of Scripture, it overcomes evil with good (Rom. 12:21).

Love Considers the Welfare of Weaker Believers

From the beginning of the Christian era, believers have fought over their freedoms in Christ. Among Jewish and Gentile Christians in Rome, intense conflicts arose over food regulations and observance of holy days. Paul describes these as conflicts over "opinions" or "disputable matters" (Rom. 14:1). By this he means their disagreements were not over fundamental doctrines but rather secondary matters of personal conscience. Christians today still quarrel over these marginal issues.

Loving leaders demonstrate great understanding of people and their problems.

Foremost among the principles Paul lays down for resolving this kind of conflict is love: "For if your brother is grieved by what you eat, you are no longer walking in love. By what you eat, do not destroy the one for whom Christ died" (Rom. 14:15). Thus love does not "injure" or "destroy" fellow believers over secondary issues such as food. Love does not seek its own advantage (1 Cor. 13:5). Love denies itself for the good of the conscience of another. As the Scripture reminds us, "Let each of us please his neighbor for his good, to build him up. For Christ did not please himself" (Rom. 15:2-3).

Love protects weak and misguided brothers and sisters (Rom. 14:15). The lifestyle of love requires a believer to put aside legitimate exercise of one's liberties for the spiritual welfare of a weak believer. Love says, "if food makes my brother stumble, I will never eat meat, lest I make my brother stumble" (1 Cor. 8:13). Pride and selfishness, however, refuse to forgo one's rights and freedoms for the sake of a weaker believer. The loveless use of freedom is always destructive to others as well as to oneself. The scriptural answer to the misuse of Christian liberties is this: "Do not use your freedom as an opportunity for the flesh, but through love serve one another" (Gal. 5:13). As leaders and teachers, we are to model the kind of love that will sacrifice personal freedom to serve the good of others, "and not to please ourselves" (Rom. 15:1).

Love Blesses One's Enemies

Jesus teaches that there's nothing special about loving people who love you. Even those who have no love for most people often love those who love them. What is truly distinct and divine and righteous is loving those who hate you and oppose you. This kind of love, Jesus declares, makes us most like our heavenly Father:

> But I say to you, Love your enemies and pray for those who persecute you, so that you may be sons of your Father who is in heaven. For he makes his sun rise on the evil and on the good, and sends rain on the just and on the unjust. For if you love those who love you, what reward do you have? Do not even the tax collectors do the same? And if you greet only your brothers, what more are you doing than others? Do not even the Gentiles do the same? You therefore must be perfect, as your heavenly Father is perfect. (Matt. 5:44-48; also Luke 6:27-28)

Following our Lord's extraordinary teaching, Paul writes:

• Bless those who persecute you; bless and do not curse them. (Rom.12:14)

♦ If your enemy is hungry, feed him; if he is thirsty, give him something to drink [an act of kindness]; for by so doing you will heap burning coals on his head [shaming the person by kindness and thus perhaps changing his mind]. (Rom. 12:20)

It doesn't matter whether those who hate you are hostile unbelievers or believers. You are still to bless them, pray for them, show mercy to them in their need, and win them with lovingkindness. Jonathan Edwards reminds us that the very "nature of love is good-will" toward others.[5] This good will extends even to our enemies.

Love Does Not Seek Personal Retaliation or Revenge

When their feelings have been hurt, people often feel justified in doing anything they want in retaliation. They can leave the church, divide the body, explode with uncontrolled anger, cut people off, lie, hate, and backbite. They try to justify the most wicked, sinful behavior with the simple excuse, "But I've been hurt!"

Scripture prohibits the spirit of retaliation, the get-even mentality that plagues human nature, with the clear command: Repay no one evil for evil.

Scripture, however, prohibits the spirit of retaliation, the get-even mentality that plagues human nature, with the clear command: "Repay no one evil for evil" (Rom. 12:17; 1 Thess. 5:15; 1 Pet. 3:9). When insulted, we are not to return the insult; when attacked, we are not to retaliate; when criticized, we are not to slander; when hurt, we are not to strike back.

The Scripture further forbids seeking personal, private revenge or taking justice into our own hands: "Never avenge yourselves, but leave it to the wrath of God, for it is written, 'Vengeance is mine, I will repay, says the Lord'" (Rom. 12:19). It is God's prerogative to punish evil, and he will see to it. Remember, too, that he has established human government and courts to judge and punish evildoers (Rom. 13:1-7).

Rather than seeking retribution, Christians are to "overcome evil with good" (Rom. 12:21). As leaders, we are to set the example and win over evil with kindness and forgiveness, trusting in God's justice to make matters right in the end.

Why Greater Controversy Calls for Greater Love

Conflict with brothers and sisters in Christ tests the genuine depths of our love, yet we often fail to exhibit Christ's love. Francis Schaeffer, who faced plenty of controversy in his life, reminds us of what we often forget: The more difficult and potentially explosive the controversy among true believers, the greater the need to display more love, not less:

> The more serious the wrongness is, the more important it is to exhibit the holiness of God, to speak out concerning what is wrong. At the same time, the more serious the differences become, the more important it becomes that we look to the Holy Spirit to enable us to show love to the true Christians with whom we must differ. If it is only a minor difference, showing love does not take much conscious consideration. But where the difference becomes really important, it becomes proportionately more important to speak for God's holiness. And it becomes increasingly important in that place to show the world that we still love each other.
>
> Humanly we function in exactly the opposite direction: In the less important differences we show more love toward true Christians, but as the difference gets into more important areas, we tend to show less love. The reverse must be the case: As the differences among true Christians get greater, we must consciously love and show a love which has some manifestation the world may see.[6]

How naturally we revert to our old, fleshly ways (Gal. 5:20). This should not be. Conflicts provide opportunities to obey the biblical commands to love and to model love in action. Use these opportunities to grow in love and teach others to love.

Notes to Chapter 17

1. Benedict de Spinoza, *A Theologico-Political Treatise and a Political Treatise*, trans. R. H. M. Elwes (1883; reprint ed., New York: Dover, 1951), 6.
2. Francis Schaeffer, *The Mark of the Christian* (Downers Grove, Ill.: InterVarsity, 1970), 22.

3. Eph. 4:26-27, 30-31; Eph. 5:18; Gal.5:14-16, 19-26).

4. Dennis E. Johnson, "Peacemakers," appendix in John M. Frame, *Evangelical Reunion* (Grand Rapids, Mich.: Baker, 1991), 171.

5. Jonathan Edwards, *Charity and Its Fruits* (1852; reprint ed., Edinburgh: Banner of Truth, 1978), 196.

6. Schaeffer, *The Mark of the Christian,* 27.

Chapter 18

Obeying Christ's Commands and Teaching Others to Obey

If you love me, you will keep my commandments.
John 14:15

As a young child, Helen Keller completely lost her sight and hearing. How she developed from an uncontrollable, frightened, deaf-blind child into an intelligent, gracious woman who authored fourteen books and was respected by leaders around the world has been recorded in her book, *The Story of My Life*, and a full-length movie, *The Miracle Worker*.

At first, it seemed impossible to teach language and discipline to Helen Keller, a child living in a world of silent darkness. But her teacher, Anne Sullivan, was doggedly determined to teach her language. Their relationship began with a war of wills. Helen ate with her hands and grabbed food from other people's plates. At times, she would lie on the floor, kicking and screaming. When Anne tried to discipline her, she would pinch and scream. Out of this nearly impossible situation, Anne Sullivan taught her language and love. In a letter to a friend, Anne Sullivan reveals the secret "gateway" to educating and loving Helen:

> I suppose I shall have many such battles with the little woman before she learns the only two essential things I can teach her, obedience and love.[1]
>
> I very soon made up my mind that I could do nothing with Helen in the midst of the family, who have always allowed her to do exactly as she pleased. She has tyrannized everybody ... and like all tyrants she holds tenaciously to her divine right to do as she pleases.... I saw

clearly that it was useless to try to teach her language or anything else until she learned to obey me. I have thought about it a great deal, and the more I think, the more certain I am that obedience is the gateway through which knowledge, yes, and love, too, enter the mind of the child.[2]

Anne Sullivan, an exceptionally gifted teacher, understood the significance of obedience in the process of education. She saw the connection between obedience and love. We, too, must recognize that faithful obedience is essential to growth in the Christian life and to effective Christian leadership.

Connecting Love and Obedience

As teachers and leaders of God's people, we must understand that our obedience or disobedience affects many people for good or evil—even whole churches and denominations. Obedience and love are directly connected throughout Scripture. Let's look briefly at what the Bible says about the connection between the two.

Obedience Is Required

The Scripture commands us to love God, our neighbor, our fellow believers, our enemies, and all people. These are not merely suggestions; they are commands. Therefore we have an obligation to love God and to love our neighbor. John emphasizes this obligation and duty when he writes, "we ought" to lay down our lives for one another (1 John 3:16). Alexander Ross summarizes the point well:

> **Our obedience or disobedience affects many people for good or evil.**

> Love is not an emotion to which we may give expression now and then, as we feel inclined; it is a *duty* required of us at all times by God, and the children of God ought surely to obey their Heavenly Father.[3]

Obedience Expresses Love for God

One of the most important ways we express love for God is by obeying him. John makes it clear: "For this is the love of God [love for God], that we keep his commandments" (1 John 5:3). Loving God is associated with keeping His commandments in the Old Testament as well.[4]

Jesus Christ is the supreme example of this important truth: "I do as the Father has commanded me, so that the world may know that I love the Father" (John 14:31). Bruce Ware writes, "Jesus wants others to know of his love for the Father through the very obedience ... that he so gladly and uncompromisingly performs."[5] Jesus' obedience to his Father was obedience "to the point of death, even death on a cross" (Phil. 2:8). We, too, now express love for God and love for Christ by our willing and complete obedience. In the words of our Lord Jesus, "Whoever has my commandments and keeps them, he it is who loves me" (John 14:21).

Obedience Evidences Our Love for God

John teaches that the evidence and assurance we know God and love God is obedience to his Word: "And by this we know that we have come to know him, if we keep his commandments.... But whoever keeps his word, in him truly the love of God [love for God] is perfected [it is fully what it should be]" (1 John 2:3, 5). Our love for Christ is evidenced by our obedience to Christ: "Whoever has my commandments and keeps them, he it is who loves me" (John 14:21). Obedience demonstrates love for God. Disobedience, on the other hand, betrays an absence of love: "Whoever does not love me," Jesus says, "does not keep my words" (John 14:24).

Obedience Is a Condition for Enjoying Fellowship with Christ

To his disciples, Jesus says, "If you keep my commandments, you will abide in my love, just as I have kept my Father's commandments and abide in his love" (John 15:10). We do not merit Christ's love by our works or earn salvation by obedience, but obedience is necessary for enjoying and growing in close fellowship with Christ. This principle is expressed in the words of an old hymn "Trust and Obey," by John Sammis: "Trust and obey, for

there's no other way to be happy in Jesus but to trust and obey." The disobedient believer, on the other hand, forfeits this joy.

Jesus himself is the supreme example of this vital truth. While on earth,
he was the obedient Son. He enjoyed and remained in his Father's love
through obedience to his Father's commandments (John 10:17; 14:31, 15:10).
Now Jesus wants his disciples to "abide" in his love through obedience to
his commands. Bruce Ware sheds light on the reasoning of our Lord when
he writes,

> But, in order for [the disciples] to know that the connection between
> obedience and abiding in the love of the one whom they are to obey
> is not new, or strange, or particular only to them, he makes clear
> that this is exactly how things have worked between himself (the
> Son) and his Father.... Love and obedience, then, run together in an
> inseparable union in this relationship between God the Father and
> God the Son.[6]

Obedience Is a Fruit of Love

The nature of Christian love is to do the will of God. Obeying the Father
was a delight for Jesus because he loved his Father: "I do as the Father has
commanded me, so that the world may know that I love the Father" (John
14:31). When we love Christ, we love his teachings. We love to please him,
and we do his will because that is what pleases our beloved.

"If you love me," Jesus says, "you will keep my commandments" (John
14:15). Jesus is speaking in this verse of willing obedience from the heart,
not a forced or joyless obedience. Love motivates us to obey, and the Holy
Spirit empowers us to love (John 14:15-31; also see Deut. 30:6).

Christian Leaders Are in the
Obedience Business

Jesus Christ and his apostles were obedient servants who showed others how
to love and obey God. The same is true of Christian leaders and teachers
today. We are in the business of teaching and modeling obedience to
God.

Teaching Others to Obey

The Great Commission states: "Go therefore and make disciples of all nations … teaching them to observe [obey] all that I have commanded you" (Matt. 28:19-20). Instructing people to obey Christ's commands is part of the Great Commission. It's not enough to teach the facts about Christ, we are to teach, exhort, and train disciples to obey and live according to the commands of Christ.

> Leaders who think that growth in grace comes by knowing the Word of God without doing it will produce congregations of passive Christians which resemble human beings that eat too much and exercise too little.[7]

So our teaching ministries, whether at home, in church, or at a theological institution, are to be aimed at promoting obedience to Christ. Sometimes we overlook these aspects of ministry. While I was attending seminary, I saw students who spent several hours a day in class and in the study of the Bible and theology, but did not attend church or share their faith, had no ministry responsibilities, and whose lifestyles were no different than those of unbelievers. They enjoyed the study of theology and found the Bible interesting on a theoretical level, but they did not apply what they learned, nor did they experience life transformation. This is not Jesus' idea of education or disciple making. He said to go and make disciples, teaching them to obey "all that I have commanded you" (Matt. 28:20).

We are in the business of teaching and modeling obedience to God.

Jesus also warned of the dangers of calling him "Lord" and hearing his Word but failing to obey it or put it into practice (Matt. 7:21-23; Luke 6: 46-49; 8:21).

Modeling Obedience

In a world that reeks of rebellion against God, people need to see living examples of obedience to his Word. Indeed, people learn as much by watching the lives of their leaders as by listening to their words. Many forces—sin, Satan, the flesh, the world, and our own laziness—continually tempt us to disobey God's will, but godly examples of obedience inspire and encourage us to obey.

Two outstanding Old Testament examples of leaders who modeled and taught obedience are Ezra and Nehemiah. When Ezra, a teacher, priest, and scribe, arrived in Jerusalem from Persia to minister to the exiles, he found that the nation's leaders had led God's people into intermarriage with foreign nations. This sin was strictly prohibited by the law of God (Ezra 9: 1-2; 10:18).

Ezra, like all proactive leaders, took immediate action. He first led the nation in confession and repentance (Ezra 9:3–10:1). Then he laid out an action plan to reverse their sinful choices, and the people responded in obedience.

Ezra was not only a teacher but an obedient practitioner of the truth. He "set his heart to study the Law of the Lord, *and to do it* and to teach his statutes and rules in Israel" (Ezra 7:10; italics added). His teaching and reform would have been powerless were it not for his sterling example of obedience.

Later, Nehemiah arrived in Jerusalem from Persia to rebuild the fallen walls of the city of Jerusalem, destroyed by the Babylonians a hundred and forty years earlier. As Ezra did before him, Nehemiah had to exhort the nation's leaders to obey the law of God.

Some of the leaders were exploiting their own people's desperate economic situation in direct disobedience of the Old Testament laws of usury (Neh. 5:7-13). Nehemiah rebuked their greed and set a good example for them to follow. He used his own money to redeem Israelites who had been enslaved because of debt. He gave loans to the poor.

Nehemiah is one of the great leaders portrayed in the Old Testament, a model of loving obedience to the will and the law of God.

As governor of Judea, he did not take his full monetary allowance from the king. He did not burden the people with undue taxes. Instead, he helped to feed people and lighten their burdens.

Nehemiah is one of the great leaders portrayed in the Old Testament, a model of loving obedience to the will and the law of God. Because of his faithfulness, wisdom, and love, the people obeyed God and prospered. He is an example for us today.

A Leader's Obedience or Disobedience Affects Others

The Old Testament kings of Israel illustrate the blessings of a leader's obedience and the calamities of a leader's disobedience. During the era of Israel's kings, some 460 years from the anointing of King Saul to the Babylonian captivity (586 BC), a pattern emerges that can be described in one sentence: As the king goes, so goes the nation.

Disobedient Kings

Some of Israel's kings blatantly disobeyed God's law. They sacrificed to pagan idols, defiled the temple, disregarded Passover and Sabbath, violated the covenant, lost the written law, rejected God's prophets, and brought the nation to the point of spiritual ruin and divine judgment. These leaders did not love the Lord their God with all their heart and soul and might (Deut. 6:4-5), nor did they teach the people to love God and keep his commandments (Deut. 6:7-9). Since they did not love or trust God, they did not obey him. Instead, they loved and obeyed the gods of other nations.

Like the disobedient kings of Israel, some Christian theologians and church officials lead people into false doctrine and sexual immorality in the name of tolerance. They call evil good and good evil, saying that a loving God would not judge people. They reinterpret Christian words and doctrines to make them compatible with the idols of our secular culture. It's a tragedy, but Israel's history of disobedience is repeated today among many professing Christians.

Half-Hearted Kings

Some kings turned their backs on God; others were half-hearted in their obedience to God. They made partial reforms, trusted the Lord when it suited their purposes, and they compromised the worship of Yahweh by leaving intact the high places of idolatrous worship. In the end, they left a poor legacy for themselves and permitted the nation to drift further from God.

A clear example of the results of disobedience comes from the life of King Saul in the Old Testament. God instructed the king to completely destroy the city of Amalek, including all of its animals. But Saul obeyed only partway: He destroyed the city but saved the best animals and goods for himself and the people. When the prophet Samuel confronted him for disobeying the Lord, Saul justified his disobedience by claiming that the animals had been saved for religious sacrifices to God. Samuel's response is piercing:

> Has the Lord as great delight in burnt offerings and sacrifices, as in obeying the voice of the Lord? Behold, to obey is better than sacrifice, and to listen than the fat of rams. For rebellion is as the sin of divination, and presumption is as iniquity and idolatry. (1 Sam. 15:22-23)

If we were honest with ourselves, we would have to admit that many of the problems and conflicts we face in our local churches can be traced to this kind of half-hearted obedience to God's Word. Many fights and divisions within the church result from disobedience of basic biblical rules of conduct. Christians gossip and slander, seek personal revenge, sue one another, and refuse to forgive and be reconciled. Such disobedience leads to divisions within our churches, broken relationships, and bitter, disillusioned believers. We wonder why our churches are weak and troubled. The reason is simple: We reap what we sow (Gal. 6:7-8).

Obedient Kings

While there were many disobedient kings, there were also some good kings who loved the Lord and obeyed him wholeheartedly. King Josiah, the Scripture says, "turned to the Lord with all his heart and with all his soul and with all his might, according to all the Law of Moses" (2 Kings 23: 25). This is another way of saying he obeyed the command to "love the Lord your God with all your heart and with all your soul and with all your might" (Deut. 6:5).

Out of wholehearted love for the Lord and obedience to his Word, Josiah destroyed the idols of Baal and banished the false prophets, removed the high places of idolatrous worship, cleansed the city of Jerusalem of its foreign objects of worship, and rid the land of mediums and male cult prostitutes. He also restored the temple to the worship of Yahweh, reinstituted the priests, and recovered the lost book of the law of Moses. In response to hearing the words of the law, Josiah humbled himself and did according to all that was written in it (2 Kings 22:11, 13). He renewed the covenant with God; led the people in prayer, confession, and repentance; taught the law of God; and reinstituted the yearly celebration of the Passover (2 Kings 22:1–23:25).

Josiah loved the Lord his God with all his heart, soul, and might. Thus he sought to obey fully all that the Lord had commanded in his law. This brought revival and reformation to the whole nation. All subsequent reformations and revivals have begun the same way, with a heart moved by the Holy Spirit to love and obey the Word of the Lord.

Obedience-oriented Leadership

One of the greatest blessings a church can experience is for its leaders and teachers to love the Lord and delight in obeying his Word. It thrills the heart to see a church where the leaders are committed to obeying Scripture, eager to seek God's will, and determined to lead the church in ways that please the Lord. Such leaders are better leaders because they are far less inclined to neglect their God-given pastoral duties.

Obedience is a powerful motivation. Obedient leaders will love and serve their fellow believers sacrificially because the Scripture says "we ought to lay down our lives for the brothers" (1 John 3:16). And they are willing to confront sinful behavior because the Scripture says "reprove, rebuke, and exhort, with complete patience and teaching" (2 Tim. 4:2). They will lead more diligently because the Scripture says that those who lead are to lead "with zeal" (Rom. 12:8). They will work to feed and care for God's flock because they believe that the Holy Spirit has placed them in the church to shepherd the flock (Acts 20:28). They will fulfill their responsibilities because they are obedient servants.

> One of the greatest blessings a church can experience is for its leaders and teachers to love the Lord and delight in obeying his Word.

Practitioners of Love

If we do not teach and model obedience, we will not teach and model Christian love. We cannot rightly talk about love without addressing obedience. Love can grow only if it is rooted in the soil of true obedience.

The Bible says, "Be doers of the word, and not hearers only, deceiving yourselves" (James 1:22). If we hear the words of God but do not obey them, we are self-deceived and his words have no lasting transforming power over us (James 1:22-25). Merely hearing God's words about love is not sufficient. We must set our minds on being eager "doers of the word." Biblical commentator R. V. G. Tasker reminds us that "Christianity is essentially a life to be lived."[8]

It isn't enough to hear and agree with the Bible's teaching on love. We must be practitioners of biblical love. Only those who hear *and do* are "blessed," says James, not those who sit in church and hear but immediately forget (James 1:25). James's instruction comes from our Lord himself: "Blessed … are those who hear the word of God and keep it" (Luke 11:28). "If you know these things, blessed are you if you do them" (John 13:17).

Notes to Chapter 18

1. Helen Keller, *The Story of My Life: The Restored Edition*, ed. James Berger (New York: Modern Library, 2003), 223.
2. Ibid., 223-24.
3. Alexander Ross, *The Epistles of James and John*, NICNT (Grand Rapids, Mich.: Eerdmans, 1954), 208.
4. Ex. 20:6; Deut. 10:12-13; 11:1, 13, 22; 19:9; 30:16, 19-20. Leon Morris comments, "there is a marked reluctance to see obedience to God's commands as a response of love. We tend to assume that obedience to a code has little to do with love. But the men of the Old Testament did not see things this way." *Testaments of Love* (Grand Rapids, Mich.: Eerdmans, 1981), 58.
5. Bruce A. Ware, *Father, Son, and Holy Spirit* (Wheaton, Ill.: Crossway, 2005), 86.
6. Ware, *Father, Son, and Holy Spirit*, 86-87.
7. Kenneth B. Mulholland, "Teaching Them … All Things: Three Dots and a Pilgrimage," in *Teaching Them Obedience in All Things: Equipping for the 21ˢᵗ Century*, ed. Edgar J. Elliston (Pasadena, Calif.: William Carey Library, 1999), 10.
8. R. V. G. Tasker, *The General Epistle of James*, TNTC (Grand Rapids, Mich.: Eerdmans, 1957), 51.

Appendix of Biblical Greek Words

Most Christians are familiar with the Greek noun for love, *agapē,* but are not as familiar with the other words for love found in both the Greek Old and New Testaments. This brief overview is included here to provide a fuller understanding of—and to correct mistaken notions about—the Greek words for love.

Greek Words for Love in the Septuagint

The Old Testament was written in Hebrew, with a few portions in Aramaic.[1] But between 250 BC and 150 BC the Hebrew Scriptures were translated into Koine Greek. This Greek translation is called the Septuagint and is often abbreviated by the Roman numerals LXX, meaning seventy. The Septuagint as we have it today comprises both the divinely inspired Hebrew Scriptures (our canonical Old Testament) and the Apocrypha[2] (noninspired books, but nonetheless important historical works).

The New Testament writers and the first Christians read and were most familiar with the Greek Old Testament (the Septuagint). The writers of the New Testament regularly quoted from it. J. Julius Scott states, "Eighty percent of the Old Testament quotations in the New Testament are taken from the Septuagint."[3] He goes on to say that "the Septuagint became the Bible of the early church."[4]

In the Septuagint the predominant Greek verb for love, *agapaō*, appears 271 times.[5] So *agapaō* was not a new word invented by the New Testament writers. In fact, not only is it the dominant word for love in the Septuagint, in the first century AD it had become the regular, general word for love used among Greek-speaking people.

In the Septuagint *agapaō* is used for all kinds of expressions of love including, and most significant, God's love for his people and their love for him. This usage of the word in the Septuagint made *agapaō* a ready word for the New Testament writers to use in expressing God's love, love for God, and love among members of the family of God.

The other major Greek verb for love in the Septuagint is *phileō*. Although it was the more dominant verb for love in the classical Greek language, it is used only thirty-two times in the Septuagint (written in Koine Greek), and mostly in reference to kissing. In a few instances it is used interchangeably with *agapaō*. *Phileō* is never used in the Septuagint for God's love for his people or their love for God. Its noun form, *philia,* can denote love but most often is used in the Septuagint for friendship.

The noun for love, *agapē*, with which we are most familiar today because of its frequent New Testament use, appears in the Septuagint only nineteen times. Eleven of these usages of *agapē* appear in the Song of Solomon. Below are a few examples of *agapē* in the canonical Old Testament. In all of them *agapē* is used in reference to sexual love:

- The hatred with which [Amnon] hated [Tamar] was greater than the love [*agapē*] with which he had loved [*agapaō*] her. (2 Sam. 13:15)
- He brought me to the banqueting house, and his banner over me was love. (Song 2:4)
- For love is strong as death. (Song 8:6)
- Many waters cannot quench love.... If a man offered for love all the wealth of his house, he would be utterly despised. (Song 8:7)

In the Apocrypha *agapē* is used for love of wisdom that leads to God, love for God, and possibly even God's love for his people.

- And love of her [wisdom] is the keeping of her laws, and giving heed to her laws is assurance of immortality, and immortality brings one near to God. (Wisd. Sol. 6:18-19)

◆ Those who trust in him will understand truth, and the faithful will abide with him in love [in their love for God or in God's love for them]. (Wisd. Sol. 3:9)
◆ Blessed are those who saw [God], and those who have been adorned in love [human love or God's love]; for we also shall surely live. (Ecclus. or Sir. 48:11)

The adjective *agapētos*, which is the Greek word for "beloved," appears twenty-four times in the Septuagint; the noun *agapēsis*, "love," thirteen times. This word is not used in the New Testament. Thus the words from the *agapaō* word group appear 327 times in the Septuagint.

Greek Words for Love in the New Testament

The Greek words *agapaō, agapē,* and *agapētos*—the primary word group used to express Christian love—appear a total of 320 times in the New Testament. The verb *agapaō* appears 143 times. Its religious and theological use in the Septuagint made it a natural choice for the New Testament writers. Christ's teaching on love and his extraordinary example of love, moreover, gave the word fresh meaning.

In nonbiblical Greek literature before the second and third centuries AD the noun *agapē* appears rarely, if at all. In the Septuagint the noun *agapē* appears nineteen times, mainly in reference to physical, sensual love, and possibly once or twice in reference to God's love for his people. In contrast, *agapē* appears 116 times in the New Testament, most frequently used by Paul (seventy-five times) and John (thirty times). The first Christian writers made this sparsely used noun for love *(agapē)* the common term for expressing the love of God and of Christ as well as human love. Of course, *agapē*'s obvious relation to its verb form *agapaō* helped in this choice, and other Greek nouns for love simply were not suitable. *So the first Christians used the noun* agapē *and filled it with their rich concept of love as revealed in Christ's teaching and cross. This gave the word its distinctive Christian significance and meaning.*

The Greek adjective *agapētos* is the word for "beloved," or one who is loved. In the New Testament *agapētos* is used sixty-one times, twenty-seven of those by Paul. Jesus Christ is called the "beloved Son" and believers are "beloved" of God (Rom. 1:7). Also, believers often refer to one another as "beloved," emphasizing the intimate, loving family relationship that exists among them.

In addition to the verb *agapaō* there is another verb for love, *phileō*. *Phileō is* the second most frequently used word for love in the New Testament (twenty-five times), used mostly by John in his gospel. Despite distinctions between *agapaō* and *phileō*, depending on context, the verbs are sometimes used interchangeably with no apparent difference.[6] *Phileō* as well as *agapaō* can be used in reference to different kinds of love. *Phileō* is used for the act of kissing, love between friends, the love of the Father for the Son (John 5:20), and our love for Jesus Christ (1 Cor. 16:22). But clearly, *agapaō* is the predominant word for love in the New Testament, especially in reference to God's love that makes possible our love for one another.

Finally, the New Testament uses the compound Greek word *philadelphia*, "brotherly love," a familial term, to describe the quality of love that unites Christians.[7] This kind of love is an intimate, enduring family love. The first Christians understood themselves to be a true family of brothers and sisters in Christ. As to the crucial importance of this type of love in the church, James Moffatt remarks that "no church has any prospect of stability or chance of existence in the sight of God if it neglects brotherly love."[8]

Notes

1. Ezra 4:8-6:18; 7:12-26; Dan. 2:4-7:28; Jer. 10:11.
2. The apocryphal books were written between the close of the Old Testament era and the birth of Christ. They were not a part of the Hebrew canon of Scriptures. The primary books are: 1–2 Esdras, Judith, Tobit, 1–4 Maccabees, Odes, Wisdom of Solomon, Sirach, Psalms of Solomon, Baruch, Epistle of Jeremiah, Susanna, and Bel and the Dragon.
3. J. Julius Scott Jr., *Jewish Backgrounds of the New Testament* (Grand Rapids, Mich.: Baker, 1995), 135.
4. Ibid., 136.
5. Figures from Accordance Bible Software: Oak Tree Software, 498 Palm Springs Drive, Suite 100, Altamonte Springs, FL 32701. Copyright © 2004. http://www.OakSoft.com; 877-399-5855.

6. See W. Günther and H.-G. Link, "Love," in *The New International Dictionary of New Testament Theology*, 2:538, 542.

7. The noun *philadelphia*, "brotherly love," appears in Rom. 12:10; 1 Thess. 4: 9; Heb. 13:1; 1 Peter 1:22; 2 Peter 1:7. The adjective *philadelphos*, appears in 1 Peter 3:8.

8. James Moffatt, *Love in the New Testament* (London: Hodder and Stoughton, 1929), 244.

General Index of Names

Adams, Jay E. 72
Ananias and Sapphira 13
Arnot, Anthony C. 143
Augustine 45
Arulappan, John Christian 34
Barnabas 50, 65, 126, 141
Barnett, Paul 33, 155
Barrett, C. K. 83
Bourke, Dale Hanson 114
Bredfeldt, Gary J. 133
Bridges, Jerry 15
Broomhall, A. J. 29, 61, 121
Bruce, A. B. 139
Bruce, F. F. 118
Burnham, Jonathan D. 44
Carmichael, Amy 21, 23, 31, 56
Carson, D. A. 15, 25, 72, 117-18, 120, 122
Cedar, Paul A. 95
Chambers, Oswald 31
Chapman, Robert C. 19, 26-27 43, 46, 50, 71-72
Clinton, Robert 132
Conti, Joseph G. 164
Conyers, A. J. 160, 162
Cranmer, Thomas 45
Dann, Robert B. 33
Darby, John Nelson 43
David 31, 49-50, 74, 77
Day, Richard Ellsworth 8

Denny, James 33-34, 157-58
Dorsett, Lyle W. 58-59, 162
Drummond, Henry 68
Dudley-Smith, Timothy 66, 96
Edwards, Jonathan 15, 56, 67, 69, 86, 112, 172
Elliot, Elisabeth 74
Fee, Gordon D. 78
Felix, Marcus Minucius 95
Garland, David E. 47, 72
Gosin II, Thomas S. 100
Graham, Billy 52
Green, Michael 2-3, 102
Groves, Anthony Norris 33-34
Grubb, Norman 28
Günther, W. 189
Hall, V. A. 105
Hendricks, Howard 128, 132-33, 169
Hiebert, D. Edmond 118-19
Hoehner, Harold 28
Hogg, Wilson Thomas 130
Holmes, Frank 19, 127
Hostetler, Bob 164
Houghton, Frank L. 22, 31
Howe, Reuel L. 110, 145
Hughes, Philip E. 33, 156
Ingatius 14

continued on page 192

General Index

continued from page 191

Scripture Index

continued on page 194

193

Scripture Index

continued from page 193

continued on page 196

continued on page 198

Scripture Index

continued from page 197

continued on page 200

Scripture Index

continued from page 199